LOVE, WAR, AND BRAIN CONTROL

HELEN M. RHINEHART

ABSTRACT

Aggressive and mating behaviors, crucial for survival, are inherently programmed in the brain and are orchestrated by genetically defined cell types within subcortical circuits. Despite the hard-wired nature, females exhibit a remarkable ability to flexibly adjust these behaviors to according to their reproductive states. The neural mechanisms governing the stable control and adaptive regulation of these behaviors remained unclear. Moreover, given the inherently complex and dynamic nature social interactions, the dynamics of the underlying motivational states and their encoding in the female brain was largely unknown.

Addressing these knowledge gaps in my book, I initially undertook a dissection of the subcortical circuits and genetically defined cell types involved in the control of female aggressive and mating behaviors. Using single-cell RNA sequencing and optogenetic perturbations, I identified distinct transcriptomic cell types in the ventromedial hypothalamus: α cells governing mating and ß cells regulating aggression. Furthermore, longitudinal monitoring of their activity during the transition from virginity to motherhood revealed that ß cells became more responsive to social cues, resulting a shift from mating to aggression. In a second line of investigation, I delved into the dynamics of female mating and its neural encoding. By monitoring single-cell activity in receptive females and applying dynamical system modeling to neural activity, I uncovered that α cell formed line attractor dynamics, encoding a sexual aroused state during mating. Additionally, longitudinal monitoring of activity across different hormonal states revealed population dynamics displaying receptivity state-dependent patterns across the estrus cycle. A third aspect of my research explored comprehensive changes in gene expression patterns in circuits influenced by hormones. Through comparative analysis of transcriptomic profiles in the ventromedial hypothalamus at different hormonal states. I identified qualitative changes in cell types within mating-activated α cells, correlated with sexual receptivity. These studies significantly contribute to our understanding of the neural basis controlling aggressive and mating behaviors, shedding light on their flexible regulation by physiological conditions in females.

Table of Contents

Chapter 1

INTRODUCTION

The objective of this chapter is to provide an overview of my book, focusing on the neural control of mating and aggression in female mice. Social behaviors, such as mating and aggression, and their underlying neural mechanisms, exhibit significant sexual dimorphism. However, research on these topics has traditionally centered on male subjects, leading to a biased understanding of the fundamental mechanism. Many established insights are based on and generalized from male-biased results. Therefore, it is imperative to meticulously compare male and female subjects to establish equivalent understandings in females.

Chapter 1 sets the stage by offering background information and walking through a series of questions: What is known about mating and aggressive behaviors in female rodents compared to male? What is the neural circuit control? How can these behaviors in females be flexibly regulated by reproductive states? To bridge this knowledge gap, my book focuses on a critical brain region recognized as the hub for both mating and aggression circuits – the ventrolateral subdivision of ventromedial hypothalamus (VMHvl). In chapter 2, I identified two genetically distinct and specific cell types that causally control mating and aggression in females, respectively. A comparative analysis of female cell types and functions in this crucial region to previous, juxtaposed with previous male data, sheds light on the molecular and cellular mechanism underlying the sexual dimorphism of mating and aggression. Additionally, I explore how lactational states modulate aggression in mothers. Chapter 3 delves into an investigation of how estrus states regulate mating receptivity in females. Chapter 4 explores comprehensive changes in gene expression patterns in the key region led by reproductive states, highlighting remaining questions that need to be addressed. This research rectifies the existing bias in understanding by providing a more balanced and comprehensive examination of the neural control of mating and aggression in female mice.

Aggression and mating in female and male rodents

Aggression and mating are fundamental behaviors crucial for survival in rodents. According to Tinbergen's theory, both are reproductive behaviors, evolutionarily conserved, innate, stereotypical[1]. In the brain, they are hard-wired and controlled by genetically defined cell types within subcortical circuits[2–7].

Aggressive behaviors

Despite the necessity of aggression for the survival of both sexes, it exhibits sexual dimorphism. The prevalence of aggression is higher in males due to selective pressures linked to limited mating opportunities[8]. In various rodent species, such as mice, rats and hamsters, female and male express aggression in quantitatively similar ways, primarily using biting as their main strategy to harm an opponent[9]. While both sexes bite, fine differences in biting patterns exist. For example, female mice and rats tend to attack female intruders on their back and male intruders on vulnerable body parts, while resident male mice bite male intruders on both their back and head[10].

Recent studies have revealed significant sex differences in reactive vs. appetitive aggression. Males exhibit more wrestling and less investigative behavior, will work for access to a subordinate to attack and find aggression rewarding. Females, on the other hand, display more bites, readily alternate between aggressive and investigative behaviors, but do not find aggression rewarding[11]. Notably, a substantial difference is that aggression in female is periodic, occurring only or enhanced during the maternal period, while in males, it is not[12–14]. This distinction highlights the sex-specific expression and modulation of aggressive behaviors to meet the distinct needs of each sex. I will expand this point later.

Mating behaviors

Female mating behaviors differ qualitatively different from males. Mating can be categorized into appetitive and consummatory phases[15]. In mice, the appetitive phase involves males emitting ultrasonic vocalizations (USVs) upon detecting the female's odor, followed by approaching and investigating the female's face and external genitalia. The consummatory phase includes stereotyped actions such as male mounting and pelvic movement for intromission. If the female is receptive, she assumes the "lordosis" posture, facilitating rhythmic intromissions leading to ejaculation, marking the end of the consummatory phase[16,17]. Importantly, mating behaviors in female are periodic, modulated by hormonal states, whereas in males, they are not. This distinction in periodicity further emphasizes the sex-specific regulation of mating behaviors in rodents. I will expand this point later.

Neural circuits of aggression and mating

The hypothalamus, which prevailing views regarded as hard-wired, exhibits sexually dimorphic circuitry, with the male circuits receiving more attention than its female counterpart.

Aggression circuit

Chemosensory cues, initially detected by vomeronasal receptors in the nose, relay to the hypothalamus through the olfactory bulb and amygdala, orchestrating subsequent motor actions in the midbrain[9,18]. Figure 1 provides an overview of our current understanding of brain regions that influencing male and female aggression.

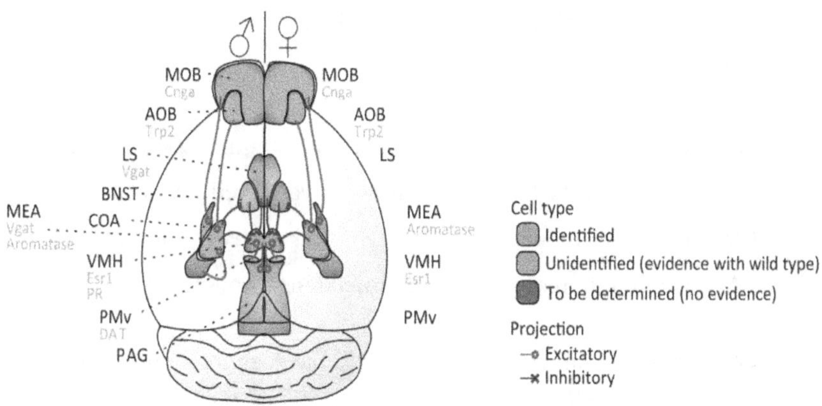

Figure 1: Aggression circuit nodes and cell types in male and female mice. (Adapted from Hashikawa *et. al.*, 2018, The Neural Mechanisms of Sexually Dimorphic Aggressive Behaviors, *Trends in Genetics*)

Rodents heavily depend on olfactory cues for triggering aggression, wherein the main olfactory bulb (MOB) and accessory olfactory bulb (AOB) play distinct roles[19–22]. The MOB primarily detects volatile cues, while the AOB specializes in non-volatile cues or pheromones. Specific receptors in olfactory sensory neurons within the main olfactory epithelium (MOE) and vomeronasal organs (VNO) detect these cues, relaying information to the MOB and AOB.

The relayed information from olfactory bulbs influences various brain regions involved in aggression. The medial amygdala (MEA) and bed nucleus of the stria terminalis (BNST), receiving inputs from the AOB, are implicated in both male and female aggression[23–26]. GABAergic neurons in the MEA, especially those expressing aromatase, drive male aggression, while the BNST has negative effects on aggression in both sexes.

The ventrolateral part of the ventromedial hypothalamus (VMHvl) acts as a central hub for aggression, receiving inputs from the MEA and BNST[27]. While studies underscore the essential role of VMHvl in male aggression[3,28,29], recent findings reveal nuanced roles for VMHvl Esr1+ cells in females, influencing both aggression and sexual receptivity[5,6]. Sexual dimorphism is evident in the

VMHvl, with distinct compartments for mating- and aggression-related cells in females[5,6].

Implicated in aggression, the ventral premammillary nucleus (PMv)[30–32] and periaqueductal grey (PAG)[5,33,34] show elevated activity during aggression. The PMv, receiving inputs from the MEA and projecting to the VMHvl, and the PAG, a midbrain region, receive projections from the VMHvl.

The lateral septum (LS) negatively regulates aggression, suppressing activity in aggressionrelated neurons. The LS, dense in inputs from the hippocampus, potentially evaluates territoriality during agonistic encounters[35,36]. Additionally, the medial prefrontal cortex (mPFC) and medial dorsal thalamus (MD) influence aggression circuitry, with enhanced synaptic strengthening in mPFC pyramidal neurons corresponding to higher dominance rankings in male mice[37,38].

Despite a common role in both male and female aggression, sexual dimorphism is evident. Differences in size, cell number, gene expression, and responses during social behaviors between sexes are observed in the MEA and BNST. The VMHvl exhibits distinct compartments in females, while the LS displays sex-specific modulation. Overall, the basic aggression circuitry is qualitatively similar between sexes, but quantitative differences suggest a nuanced interplay between brain regions and sexual dimorphism in aggression regulation.

Within the aggression circuit, particularly the extensively studied hypothalamus, the number and distribution of aggression-related cells likely differ between sexes. In males, these cells are dispersed throughout the VMHvl, while in females, they are restricted to the medial half[5,6]. The larger size of the male VMHvl implies a higher total number of aggressionresponsive cells. This aligns with recordings showing higher activity in males, consistent with their larger dendrites and more synapses[28]. Future studies should explore additional properties of aggression-related cells, such as electrophysiological characteristics, morphology, transcriptome profiles, and synaptic inputs, which are likely to vary between sexes. Notably, my research identified a cell type causally controlling female aggression, indicating transcriptomic differences in the VMHvl between female and male mice. While a female-specific aggression-activated cell type exists and is activated by male aggression, an additional male-specific cell type is exclusively activated in males.

Mating circuit

Similar to the aggression circuit, vomeronasal receptors in the nose detect chemosensory cues, which are relayed through the olfactory bulb and amygdala to the hypothalamus and further to the midbrain for motor actions (general description of path). Figure 2 summarizes current knowledge on brain regions influencing male and female mating[17]. Notably, regions associated with male mating differ from those influencing female mating, indicating a distinct mating circuitry between sexes. This suggests a qualitative similarity in mating circuitry across male and female rodents, a reasonable assumption given the distinct motor patterns involved. For instance, the medial preoptic area (MPOA) causally controls male mating behavior, specifically mounting[4], while the VMHvl causally controls female lordosis[6,7,39,40]. My research identified female-specific cell types in the VMHvl that causally control female mating, revealing distinctions between male and female mating circuitry. The identified cell types are exclusive to females, with male mating activating a cell type in females but not activating it[6].

Reproductive state-dependent regulation

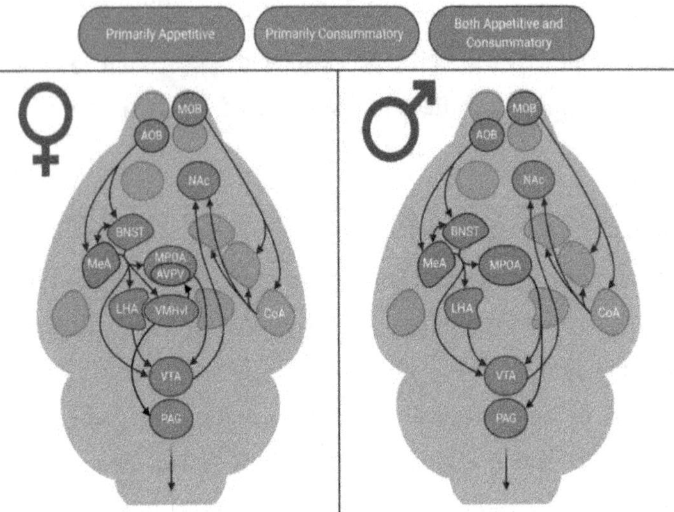

Figure 2: Mating circuit of male and female sexual behavior (Adapted from Henning et. al, 2020, Neural and Hormonal Control of Sexual Behavior, *Endocrinology*)

Stereotypical behaviors exhibit flexibility in response to physiological states, particularly in females, where adjustments are made according to reproductive states.

Lactational-state dependent regulation of aggression

Aggressive behaviors undergo changes based on lactational states. Virgin females do not display aggressive behaviors, but lactating, multiparous female mice exhibit heightened aggression, especially in the first two weeks of lactation[9,41–44] (Figure 3). This aggression declines significantly during the last week of lactation and ceases after weaning. Steroid hormones like estrogen and progesterone, as well as non-steroid hormones such as vasopressin, oxytocin, and prolactin, have been identified as regulators of maternal aggression[42–50]. However, the neural basis of their flexible regulations remained unclear. My book work revealed changes in the sensitivity of aggression-related VMHvl cells across the lactational cycle[6], shedding light on the intricate regulation of maternal aggression.

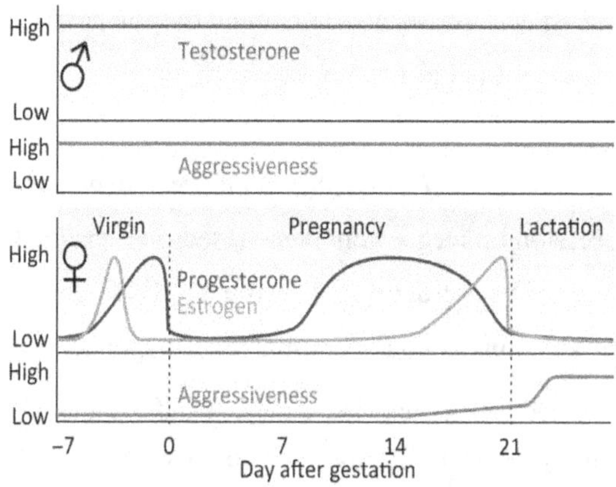

Figure 3: Circulating steroid hormones and corresponding aggression level in adult males and adult females across lactational cycle. Orchestrated changes in sex hormone levels during pregnancy are likely essential for elevating aggression during lactation in female. (Adapted from Hashikawa et al., 2018, The Neural Mechanisms of Sexually Dimorphic Aggressive Behaviors, *Trends in Genetics*)

Estrus-state dependent regulation of mating

Mating behaviors vary according to estrus states, regulated by gonadal steroid hormones[16,17,51,52]. The estrous cycle in rodents, characterized by fluctuating estrogen and progesterone levels, influences the receptivity of females to mating. Outside of the specific window during the estrous cycle, females reject mating attempts[17] (Figure 4). Recent studies have identified circuit-level mechanisms and changes in the anatomy and physiology of neurons associated with female receptivity[7,53]. One study showed that projections of PR^+

VMH neurons to the anteroventral periventricular (AVPV) nucleus change across the estrous cycle, with approximately threefold more termini and functional connections during estrus. In vivo recordings reveal reproductive-state-dependent changes in VMHvl^{Cckar+} cell spontaneous activity and responsivity, with the highest activity occurring during estrus. These in vivo response changes coincide with robust alterations in VMHvl^{Cckar+} cell excitability and synaptic inputs. To comprehensively address the dynamics of female receptivity and mating behavior, I employed miniscope imaging to observe neural representations in the female VMHvl across the estrus cycle. This approach revealed a dynamic and hormone-dependent line attractor in neural state space during mating, indicating a persistent, escalating internal state of female sexual arousal or receptivity[54].

Hormonal-state dependent regulation of gene expression

Gene expression undergoes changes based on reproductive states, with steroid hormones playing a crucial role in the VMHvl. Known expressions of *Mc4r* and *Cckar* are found to be hormonal state-dependent[55–57]. In order to obtain a comprehensive understanding, I conducted transcriptomic analysis of the female ventral VMH at different hormonal states, revealing significant changes in a vast number of genes, including those specific to hormonal states and cell types. During the course of my book research, another study conducted genetically targeted sequencing of estrogen receptor 1-expressing (*Esr1+*) populations and also identified a considerable number of genes exhibiting differential expression across estrous states. These profiles provide intricate insights into gene expression changes in response to hormonal states, encompassing the intricate interplay between genes, cell types, dynamics, and behaviors within the VMHvl.

In summary, my research explores the nuanced interplay between reproductive states, neural circuits, and gene expression, offering valuable insights into the complex regulatory mechanisms underlying aggression, mating, and gene expression in female rodents.

Chapter 2

Summary

Female mice exhibit opposing social behaviors towards males, depending on their reproductive state: virgins display sexual receptivity (lordosis behavior), while lactating mothers attack. How a change in reproductive state produces a qualitative switch in behavioral response to the same conspecific stimulus is unknown. Using single-cell RNAseq, we identify two distinct subtypes of Estrogen receptor-1 (*Esr1*)-positive neurons in the ventrolateral subdivision of the female ventromedial hypothalamus (VMHvl), and demonstrate that they causally control sexual receptivity and aggressiveness in virgins and lactating mothers, respectively. Between- and within-subject bulk calcium recordings from each subtype reveal that the aggression-specific cells acquire an increased responsiveness to social cues during the transition from virginity to maternity, while the responsiveness of the mating-specific population appears unchanged. These results demonstrate that reproductive state-dependent changes in the relative activity of transcriptomically distinct neural subtypes can underlie categorical switches in behavior associated with physiological state changes.

Introduction

Internal states can profoundly alter innate behavioral responses to releasing stimuli, but the underlying cellular and molecular mechanisms remain poorly understood. Female mice show a reproductive state-dependent switch in social behavior towards male conspecifics. Virgins exhibit sexual receptivity (lordosis) towards males [9,58], while lactating mothers exhibit aggression (and towards females as well) [41,42,59]. Maternal aggressiveness disappears after pups are weaned and another mating cycle ensues [44] (Figure 1A). This reversible behavioral switch maximizes mating opportunities for virgins while protecting pups from infanticide. Although hormones such as oxytocin and vasopressin [36,42,44], have been implicated in this behavioral switch, the underlying cellular and circuit mechanisms remain largely unknown.

In female rats, the ventrolateral subdivision of the ventromedial hypothalamus (VMHvl) is critical for lordosis behavior [39,40]. Within VMHvl, a neuronal subset that expresses the type1 estrogen receptor (*Esr1*; also known as *ERα*) was strongly but indirectly implicated in sexual receptivity (reviewed in [60]). More recent studies in mice using genetic tools demonstrated that VMHvl neurons expressing the progesterone receptor (*PR*) (which coexpress Esr1; Kim *et al.*, 2019) are essential both for female mating (Yang *et al.*, 2013; Inoue *et al.*, 2019), as well as maternal aggression (Hashikawa *et al.*, 2017). However while optogenetic activation of these VMHvl$^{Esr1+/PR+}$ cells promoted attack in lactating females, it did not promote aggression or lordosis in virgins (Lee *et al.*, 2014; Hashikawa *et al.*, 2017; Inoue *et al.*, 2019).

In both virgins and lactating dams, VMHvl$^{Esr1+/PR+}$ bulk calcium activity evoked by conspecifics is equally strong [5,53], despite the dramatic difference in the effect of optogenetic stimulation. This has suggested that state-dependent changes in the function of these neurons occurs at their synaptic terminals (Figure 1B, Model 1; Inoue *et al.*, 2019) or their downstream targets. Alternatively, changes in activity could occur among subsets of VMHvl$^{Esr1+/PR+}$ neurons that are obscured in bulk calcium imaging experiments (Figure 1B, Models 2-4).

Indirect evidence has suggested that different subsets of VMHvl^{Esr1} neurons may control mating vs. aggression in females [5]. However, a causal role for these VMHvl subpopulations in sexual receptivity or attack was not demonstrated. Recent single-cell RNA sequencing (scRNAseq) of male VMHvl has revealed that the *Esr1$^+$/PR$^+$* population comprises 6-8 distinct transcriptomic cell types which are differentially activated during specific male social behaviors (Kim *et al.*, 2019). While preliminary studies identified several femalespecific VMHvl cell types [61], their behavioral role was not investigated.

Here we identify two transcriptomic cell types in female VMHvl that causally control sexual receptivity or aggressiveness, respectively. Within-subject calcium recordings during the transition from virginity to maternity indicate that the aggression-promoting neurons undergo a dramatic increase in their responsiveness to social cues, while the mating neurons do not. Thus, changes in the relative activity of transcriptomically distinct neuronal subtypes underlie a reproductive state-dependent categorical switch in female social behavior.

Results

Distinct VMHvl transcriptomic cell types are activated during female mating and aggression.

The lactation state-dependent switch between aggression and mating is a common phenomenon in female mice [42], but the level of aggressiveness differs depending on genetic background [5] or the type of opponent. We used singly housed C57BL/6N female mice, and characterized the level of aggressive behavior in different reproductive states, using a 15-min resident-intruder assay (Figure S1). Females were sequentially tested at three distinct periods in their lactation cycle: Virgin (8-10 weeks); Lactating ("Lac," 2-5 days after parturition) and Post-lactation ("Post," 3-6 days after weaning pups), using intruder mice of both sexes (Figure S1A). In the virgin state, none of the tested females attacked either male (0/15) or female (0/21) conspecific intruders. However, almost 80% of lactating resident females displayed attack towards intruder males (11/15) and/or females (16/21). Attack behavior was almost fully abolished in the post-lactation state (Figure S1B, C).

In addition, the majority (15/21) of virgin and post-lactation (17/21) females displayed male-typical mounting and pelvic thrusting behavior towards female intruders (Figure S1D), consistent with a previous report [5]. This male-typical sexual behavior dramatically decreased in lactating state (2/21) (Figure S1D). Male mice have recently been shown to exhibit two different types of mounting behavior: reproductive (sexual) or dominance (aggressive). These can be distinguished by the presence or absence of ultrasonic vocalizations (USVs), respectively [4]. Ultrasonic recordings revealed that the mounting exhibited by virgin and postlactation females was accompanied by USVs (Figure S1E, F). The meaning of this maletypical behavior in female mice is unclear. Whatever the explanation, C57BL/6N female mice dramatically change their social behaviors and display an on-off switch in aggression regardless of intruder sex, according to their lactation state (Figure 1A).

Previously, we identified multiple VMHvl transcriptomic cell types in males [61]. Although limited profiling was also performed on female VMHvl, we did not compare females from different reproductive states or attempt to link female cell types to behavior. Here we employed activity-dependent single-cell RNA sequencing (Act-seq, 10x platform) [63] in either lactating females exhibiting attack, or in virgins exhibiting lordosis, the female-typical posture of sexual receptivity [40,64] (Figure 1C). Using unsupervised clustering, we identified 27 transcriptomic cell types (T-types) in female ventral VMH (Figure 1D). Clusters #1- #12 are VMHvl cell types, based on the differentially expressed genes (DEGs) *Esr1*, *Npy2r*, *Dlk1* (for VMHvl) and *Nr5a1* (for VMHdm / anterior VMH) (Figure S2A). These data are consistent with those reported in our previous study (Figure S3B), to which we refer the reader for discussion of our statistical analyses and their limitations [61].

To identify cell types activated during mating and/or aggression, we examined in our scRNAseq data the expression levels of 139 immediate early genes (IEGs) [61] in different Ttypes within separate cohorts of behaving and control female mice. Among several significantly up-regulated IEGs, *Fos* exhibited the highest fold-induction (Figure S2C). This analysis identified non-overlapping subsets of aggression- and mating-responding T-types in VMHvl (Figure 1E-H). Clusters #2 and #3 contained cells that were significantly activated in virgins exhibiting lordosis (Figure 1E; p<0.05 compared to home cage controls). Cluster #4 contained cells that were significantly activated in lactating females following attack (Figure 1F; p<0.05, compared to controls). Baseline *Fos* expression in the absence of an intruder did not differ between states for all VMH cell types (Figure 1G).

Previous work has shown that VMHvl contains several sex-specific T-types [61]. To determine whether clusters #2, 3 and 4 were female-specific, we computationally integrated our female scRNAseq data with a previous dataset [61] that included predominantly male- as well as some female-derived samples (Figure S3). The integration was guided by the larger of the two datasets (Methods). We found that most cells (90.18%) in the female aggression-responding T-type identified here (cluster #4) corresponded to (non-dimorphic) T-type Esr1_4 in the integrated transcriptome, which was also activated during male aggression [61]. The other male aggression-responding cell type, Esr1_7, was not found in the current female-derived dataset, consistent with our previous observation that it is male-specific [61]. Therefore, female aggression activates a non-dimorphic cell type that is also activated during male aggression (Esr1_4), while male aggression additionally activates a male-specific T-type (Esr1_7).

In contrast to the aggression-responding cell type, mating-responding cell types #2 and #3 were highly female specific (Figure S3A), comprising a large proportion (11.29%+9.93%) of VMHvl neurons in females (Figure S3B right y-axis). In contrast, cluster #10 (corresponding to cell type Dlk_1) was activated in males but not in females during mating [61]. Together these data indicated that the female-specific VMHvl cell types identified by Kim et al. (2019) are activated during lordosis, while a different (but non-dimorphic) cell type is activated during male mating.

The foregoing Act-seq data suggested the hypothesis that clusters #2/3 and #4 might function specifically in female mating vs. aggression, respectively. To test this hypothesis, we sought to gain specific genetic access to these cell types. Analysis of differentially expressed genes (DEGs) in these clusters indicated that both expressed *Esr1* at varying levels (Figure 1I, *lower* and S2A), while the NPY receptor *Npy2r* was expressed in aggression-responding (Figure 1I, *upper, orange dot*), but not in mating-responding (Figure 1I, *lower, green dot*) cell types. Overall, among clusters #1-#12 in female VMHvl, 45.7% of the cells expressed *Esr1* but not *Npy2r* (VMHvl$^{Esr1+,Npy2r-}$). 18.1% of the cells expressed both *Esr1* and *Npy2r* (VMHvl^{Npy2r+}; Figure 1J), of which 21.1% constitute aggression-activated cell type #4 (Figure S2B).

Based on these data, we designed a genetic intersectional strategy using *Npy2r^{cre}* [65] and *Esr1^{flp}* [4] mice to separately label the aggression- and mating-responding subpopulations. We used *Esr1^{flp}* and *Npy2r^{cre}* and Cre-OFF/ Flp-ON (Coff/Fon) AAVs [66,67] containing different effector genes to specifically label the mating-responding population in female VMHvl (henceforth referred to as α cells). Most Npy2r-expressing cells are also *Esr1$^+$*, therefore, we used *Npy2r^{cre}* alone to label the female VMHvl aggression-responding cell type (henceforth referred to as β cells) together with Cre-ON (Con) AAVs. Although *Npy2r* labels two other VMH T-types -- #5 and #6 – those cell types were not significantly activated above controls during either mating or aggression (Figure 1E, F and S2C). This strategy thus allowed us to independently manipulate α cells or ß cells to investigate their causal roles in mating and aggression.

VMHvl α cells control female receptivity and inhibit maternal aggression.
VMHvl and its constituent *PR$^+$* neurons (which also express *Esr1*) are necessary for female mating [29,39,53]. We therefore first tested whether optogenetic inhibition of VMHvl α (matingactivated) cells would reduce sexual behaviors in virgin females (Figure S4A-E). We expressed eNpHR [66] in α cells of ovary intact virgins, whose estrus cycle we tracked through vaginal cytology, and conducted mating tests when they were in physiological estrus (Figure S4A, B). Optogenetic silencing of α cells significantly reduced the sexual receptivity of estrus virgins during their social interactions with males as measured by lordosis (Figure S4C-E). This result indicates that the normal activity of α cells is necessary for this receptive state.

We next performed gain-of-function perturbations, by optogenetically activating α cells. In previous studies using ovariectomized, estrogen-primed (OVX-E) females, activation of VMHvl PR^+ or $Esr1^+$ neurons did not increase lordosis, perhaps because hormone priming produces a "ceiling effect" on receptivity [53]. Therefore, we tested whether selective activation of *Esr1* α cells would promote lordosis in sexually naïve ovary intact virgins, which in general displayed a much lower level of sexual receptivity [64,68].

We expressed ChR2 [66] in VMHvl α cells of virgin females, and conducted a mating test when they were physiologically in estrus or diestrus (Figure 2A, B). During estrus, control virgins occasionally (but rarely) performed lordosis. In contrast, during diestrus they strongly rejected male mounting attempts and exhibited escape, kicking and audible vocalizations (Figure 2C-F, Video S1). Strikingly, optogenetic activation of α cells (10-20Hz, 20ms pulse width) effectively enhanced the frequency of lordosis, in both estrus and diestrus virgins (Figure 2C-E, Video S1). The onset of lordosis was not time-locked to photostimulation but was initiated in response to mounting attempts by the male, suggesting that activation of α cells promotes a state of receptivity rather than the motor behavior of lordosis *per se*. Consistent with this, lordosis was not promoted by α cell activation in solitary animals or during interactions with non-mounting males or females. Thus, activation of α cells significantly enhanced female sexual receptivity during estrus, when females are naturally receptive, and induced it during diestrus (Figure 2C, F and G). These results identify, for the first time, a genetically defined VMHvl cell type whose selective activation can promote or enhance sexual receptivity in both estrus and diestrus virgin females.

Next, we examined the effect of VMHvl α cell activation on aggressive behavior in lactating dams (Figure 2H-K). We activated α cells at the moment of attack onset. Optogenetic activation of α cells rapidly abrogated attack towards female intruders (Figure 2I-K, Video S2). After the abrogation of attack, the stimulated animals continued sniffing the intruder or exhibited social disengagement (e.g., walked away) (Figure 2I, Video S2). Taken together, these data indicate that activation of VMHvl α cells has distinct behavioral effects in virgin vs. lactating females, respectively, facilitating receptivity in the former and inhibiting aggressiveness in the latter.

Activation of VMHvl ß cells evoked female aggression regardless of state.
We investigated next the causal role of VMHvl ß (aggression-activated) cells in female aggressive behaviors. We first tested if VMHvl ß cells are necessary for maternal aggression (Figure 3A-E). We silenced ß cells at the onset of attack in lactating females expressing eNpHR [69] (Figure 3A, B). Optogenetic inhibition of ß cells immediately interrupted ongoing attack, after which animals exhibited sniffing or social disengagement (Figure 3C-E), similar to the effect of activating α cells. The activity of VMHvl ß cells is therefore essential for maternal aggression.

We next tested whether optogenetic activation of ß cells was able to enhance attack in naturally aggressive lactating females (Figure S4F-J). We performed photostimulation (1020Hz, 5-20ms) when the resident was close to the intruder, but not engaged in attack. Under these conditions, activation of ß cells triggered attack virtually time-locked to the onset of photostimulation (Figure S4G), increasing the fraction of trials in which lactating females exhibited attack towards intruders of either sex (Figure S4H, I).

Previous studies reported that activating VMHvl^{Esr1+} neurons in C57BL/6 virgin/nonlactating females was unable to induce attack [3,5], a result we confirmed (Figure 3K, *Esr1*$^+$). In contrast we found, surprisingly, that activating VMHvl ß cells in virgins was able to trigger fierce time-locked attack (Figure 3G-J), towards both female and male intruders (Figure 3KM). Activating ß cells also induced male-typical mounting behavior towards intruders of both sexes, in lactating as well as in virgin females (Figure 3N and S4J), as reported previously for activating VMHvl^{Esr1+} cells [3,5]. Notably, this optogenetically evoked mounting was not accompanied by ultrasonic vocalizations (USVs), in contrast to naturally occurring female mounting (Figure S1E, F), suggesting that it may be a mild form of aggression or a dominance display [4]. Together, these data suggest that activation of VMHvl ß cells does not simply trigger a motor program of attack, but rather induces an aggressive internal state, which is expressed by multiple aggressive behaviors including attack and USV⁻ mounting.

This aggressive state can be induced even in naturally non-aggressive virgin females.

Finally, we examined the effect of optogenetically activating VMHvl ß cells on mating in virgin females, during which behavior these cells are normally not strongly activated (Figure 1E, H). Activation of ß cells immediately interrupted ongoing sexual behaviors and efficiently converted them to attack, in estrus virgins (Figure 3O, P, Video S3). Taken together, these data indicate that optogenetic activation of VMHvl ß cells exerts oppositedirection effects in females, inhibiting sexual and promoting aggressive behaviors, mirroring the dual effects of α cell activation, but with an opposite sign. As both α and ß cells are glutamatergic [61], their inhibitory effects are likely to be exerted indirectly, through as-yet unidentified GABAergic intermediate cells.

VMHvl α cells, but not ß cells in virgin females selectively respond to male cues
Having established a causal role for VMHvl α and ß cells in female sexual receptivity and aggressivity, respectively, we next investigated the dynamics of their activation during social interactions. Our Act-seq results indicated that these cells were active at some point during female mating or aggressive interactions, respectively (Figure 1E, F). However, due to their lack of temporal resolution it remained unclear during which phase(s) or feature(s) of these social interactions the cells were most strongly active. For example, does their activity mainly reflect pheromonal cues, internal states or specific motor behaviors? To resolve this question, we recorded optically bulk calcium signals

(hereafter referred to as "fiber photometry" [70]) from the VMHvl α or ß cells to examine continuously their activity dynamics during social interactions.

Initially, we investigated which stimuli activate the VMHvl α cells most strongly. First, we expressed calcium sensor GCaMP6m [66] in virgin females, and performed fiber photometry recordings from VMHvl α cells during the appetitive phase of social interactions (before the initiation of consummatory mating) (Figure 4A-C). Within a given session, we introduced a female, male or toy mouse into the female's home cage (in a randomly shuffled order), allowed them to interact freely for 3 minutes, and compared the neural responses to the different intruders. The initial encounter, defined as the first close sniffing interaction between the female resident and the intruder [4]. VMHvl α cells showed a significantly higher response during an initial encounter with a male than with either a female, or a toy mouse (Figure 4E, initial encounter).

We also measured the responses of α cells during subsequent sniffing of the intruder following the initial encounter (all sniffing bouts that were followed immediately by consummatory male mounting were excluded). We observed elevated activity during almost all bouts of sniffing males, but not during sniffing of females or the toy (Figure 4H, sniff intruder). However, the magnitude of the response during these subsequent sniff bouts was typically lower than that during the initial encounter [4]. To confirm that the male-preferred response is caused by olfactory cues, we compared α cell responses when the female was presented sequentially with samples of female urine, male urine or water (order of stimuli randomly shuffled). The α cells showed a high response to male urine, but low responses to female urine or water, during the initial sniff (Figure 4K). These results indicate that VMHvl α cells are preferentially activated by male cues, even in the absence of mating behavior.

To investigate if VMHvl ß cells also display a sex-preferred response, we performed the same fiber photometric recordings in ß cells in virgins (Figure

4D). In contrast to α cells, the responses of ß cells during the initial encounter with a male were only slightly and not significantly higher than the initial responses to females (Figure 4F). Moreover, the activity of ß cells was not significantly different during subsequent bouts of sniffing a male or female (Figure 4I). Accordingly, ß cells showed similar response to male or female urine (Figure 4L). These responses overall appeared lower than those of α cells exposed to males or male urine (cf. Figure 4E, H, K vs. 4F, I, L).

To quantitatively compare the responses of VMHvl α and ß cells to males vs. females, we calculated a "male-preference-index" (MPI) (Figure G, J and M). α cells exhibited a high MPI during the initial encounter, sniff intruder and sniff urine tests. By contrast, ß cells did not show any significant sex preference in any of the comparisons (Figure 4G, J and M). Thus, the preferential response of VMHvl$^{Esr1+/PR+}$ neurons to males reported previously [53] is due almost entirely to the activity of the α cell subpopulation.

VMHvl α cells are highly active in virgin females during mating behaviors
We next investigated if VMHvl α cells are also active during consummatory sexual behaviors in a mating interaction. During the recording session, we introduced a sexually active adult male to the female home cage and allowed the two mice to interact freely for up to 30 mins (Figure 5A). The activity of α cells dramatically increased when the female was mounted by the male and displayed lordosis behavior (Figure 5B, C). The high level of activity was sustained until the mounting bouts were finished. Notably, the responses of α cells to male mounting or intromission (consummatory phase) were significantly higher than the responses to sniffing male (appetitive phase) (Figure 5E). These results indicate that α cells are not only activated by male olfactory cues, but are even more strongly activated during the consummatory phase of mating, consistent with the results of our optogenetic stimulation experiments.

In contrast, ß cells were not active during female mating behaviors, consistent with our Actseq results. Compared with the α cells, ß cells showed very low responses at both the onset of mounting by the male or during lordosis (Figure 5F-I).

Taken together, these data indicate that in virgin females, VMHvl α cells preferentially respond to male chemosensory cues, and are activated during both the appetitive (sniffing) and consummatory (mounting or intromission) phases of female mating interaction. Conversely, ß cells display similarly weak responses to both male and female cues, and are not active during sexual behaviors.

VMHvl ß cells are highly active in lactating females during aggressive interactions. To examine how VMHvl ß cells respond during female aggressive interaction, we recorded their neural activity using fiber photometry in lactating females (Figure 6A). We observed that the activity of ß cells was high at the onset of attack or sniffing of either the female or the male intruder (Figure 6B-F). The responses to female and male intruders are both high, consistent with the similar frequency of attack towards both types of intruders (Figure S1B,

C). Around 20% of lactating females did not become aggressive (Figure S1B, C). In those non-aggressive females, the activity of ß cells at the onset of sniffing was significantly lower than the activity in aggressive females (Figure 6G, H). Moreover, even in aggressive females, the activity was significantly higher at the onset of sniffing bouts which were followed by attack, than during sniffing bouts which were not followed by attack (sniffing only) (Figure S5B, C) [71].

We also examined whether there is a correlation between IEG expression in ß cells and aggressiveness using act-seq (Figure S6H). We performed transcriptomic and IEG analysis in females that did or did not attack during social interactions. We found that the aggressionresponding cell type #4 was not significantly activated in non-aggressive females (Figure S5I-K). Together, our results indicate that female VMHvl ß cells are active during maternal aggression, regardless of intruder sex, that that their level of activity correlates with the animals level of aggressiveness.

We also examined the activity of α cells during aggressive interactions (Figure 6A). α cells showed relatively low activity at onset of attack or sniffing of either a female or male intruder (Figure 6I-M). Moreover, there was no significant difference in activity during sniffing female or male intruders whether or not it was followed by attack (unlike the case for ß cells; Figure S5D, E). A direct comparison of the activity of α cells during aggressive vs. mating behaviors towards the same social target (Figure S5F, attack male vs. mounted by male), revealed that they were significantly more active during mating behavior. Conversely, the opposite was observed for the ß cells (Figure S5F, G).

Taken together with the results of our functional perturbation experiments, these data demonstrate that female VMHvl α cells and ß cells both causally control, and are specifically active during, mating and aggressive behaviors, respectively.

Neural response of VMHvl ß cells to social cues is lactation state dependent.
The identification of distinct subsets of VMHvl neurons that specifically control female mating and aggressive behaviors raised the question of whether one or both of these populations exhibits changes in activity during the transition from the virgin to the lactating state. In principle, the switch from sexual receptivity to aggression could involve a decrease in α cell activation, an increase in ß cell activation, or a combination of both (Figure 1B). To address this question, we performed longitudinal, within-subject fiber photometric analysis of bulk calcium activity in either VMHvl α cells or ß cells in initially virgin females, and followed their activity into the lactating and post-lactation states over a 9 to 10-week period (Figure 7 and Methods).

We expressed GCaMP6m in VMHvl α or ß cells of virgin females (Figure 7A and S6A). Then we performed recording of these two cell populations during three successive epochs across their lactation cycle: virgin, lactating (lac) and post-lactation (post), and compared the level of bulk calcium activity across states within the same individuals (Figure 7B and S6B). In virgin state, GCaMP6m signals in ß cells were relatively lower during exposure to either intruder males or females, but increased significantly in lactating state (Figure 7C-F and S7A-B). This increase in signals was not due to an increase in baseline GCaMP6m expression, because it returned to levels seen in virgins when the females entered postlactation state (Figure 7C-F and S7A-B). In contrast, bulk calcium signals in VMHvl α cells during interactions with male or female intruders did not change between the virgin and lactating states (Figure S6C, D, F and G). However, the MPI of α cells for sniffing intruders was significantly lower in lactating mothers than in virgins (Figure S6H, left).

Because lactating females display a different behavioral repertoire, compared with virgins or post-lactation females, it was unclear whether the observed change in ß cell activity simply reflected this switch in behavior, or a modification of their responses to sensory cues. To discriminate those two possibilities, we used a pencil cup-protected intruder to create a nocontact interaction situation (Figure 7G-L and S7C-F). In this assay, tested females could only sniff the intruder but could not display any consummatory behaviors such as attack or lordosis.

In the no-contact interaction, ß cells still displayed a significantly higher response to either male or female intruders in lactating dams, compared to virgins or post-lactational mothers (Figure 7G-L). The sniffing pattern (Figure S7C, E) and total sniffing time (Figure S7D, F) during each session was not different in all three tested states, indicating that the higher neural activity observed in the lactating state is not simply due to a longer interaction. We also compared the neural responses to urine in females in different lactation states (Figure S7GJ). Consistent with our results using intact intruders, ß cells displayed a significantly higher response to either female or male urine in the lactating state, compared to their responses in the other states (Figure S7G-J).

These results support the idea that female VMHvl ß cells, but not α cells, display a state-dependent, reversible change in responsivity to social cues that correlates with the animal's change in behavioral response to intruders.

Discussion

Transcriptomic cell types have emerged as fundamental units of brain organization and function [72,73], but whether and how specific cell types contribute to behavioral plasticity remains unclear. We have investigated the neural control of a reproductive state-dependent switch in female social behaviors [5,29,53]. Our data demonstrate that this behavioral switch reflects a reversible change in the functional properties of distinct transcriptomic cell types. These findings reveal a role for cell type-specific regulation in the state-dependent control of social behavior, and open the way to elucidating the underlying molecular- and circuit-level mechanisms.

Identification of genetically distinct VMHvl^{Esr1} subpopulations causally controlling female mating vs. aggression

The *Esr1$^+$/PR$^+$* population in VMHvl has previously been shown to be necessary for mating and aggression in both male and female mice [3–5,29]. Indirectly data have suggested that these behaviors are controlled by different cell types [5]. Here we assign causal roles in mating or aggression to two transcriptomically distinct *Esr1$^+$* subtypes in female VMHvl. We demonstrate that these cell types are not only essential for these behaviors, but that their optogenetic activation can promote them -- even under conditions where the behaviors are not naturally expressed. For example, ß cell activation induces aggressiveness in C57BL/6 virgin females, which normally never exhibit this behavior. Indeed, prior attempts to evoke aggression in virgins by stimulation of the bulk *Esr1$^+$* population were unsuccessful [3,5]. This led some to conclude that state-dependent constraints on aggression in virgins are dominant over *Esr1$^+$* neuronal function [5]. Our results show that, to the contrary, aggression can be evoked in virgins, if a specific subtype of *Esr1$^+$* neurons is activated. We speculate that the prior failure to activate aggression by stimulation of the entire $Esr1^+$ population may reflect antagonistic interactions between α and ß cells that cancel each other out.

Similarly, prior studies showed that activation of $Esr1^+$ or PR^+ VMHvl neurons failed to enhance sexual receptivity in virgins [3,5,53]. In contrast, we show here that activation of α cells can promote receptivity in estrus virgins, and induce it in normally unreceptive diestrus virgins. Several factors may explain this discrepancy. First, our genetic intersectional strategy excluded the $Npy2r^+$ (ß cell) subset, which inhibited mating when stimulated on its own. Activation of ß cells may therefore nullify the ability of α cells to promote receptivity, when both populations are co-stimulated in the bulk $Esr1^+$ population. Second, we used intact virgins rather than OVX-E females, eliminating potential "ceiling effects" on receptivity that could obscure the effect of α cell stimulation [53]. Our results indicate that even in diestrus females, α cells can activate downstream targets that control sexual receptivity (although quantitative modulation of the efficiency of this activation likely contributes as well [53]).

Interestingly, while activation of α cells could override the lack of sexual receptivity during diestrus, it was not able to do so in lactating females exposed to male intruders (Figure S4K). This was not due to an intrinsic inability to activate α cells in mothers, because their stimulation inhibited aggression. Several possibilities may explain the different behavioral phenotypes of α cell activation in virgins vs. lactating females. One is that the high level of endogenous ß cell activity in dams might antagonize the ability of α cell activation to promote receptivity. Another is that the intrinsic cellular properties of α cells or their downstream targets might be different in lactating females vs. virgins. Further studies will be required to distinguish these alternatives.

State-dependent changes in the stimulus-responsivity of female VMHvl aggression neurons If optogenetic activation of ß cells can evoke aggression in virgin females, why are virgins not naturally aggressive? Our calcium recordings indicate that in virgins, ß cells are much less responsive to male cues than are α cells. Longitudinal within-subject recordings revealed that ß cells dramatically increase their responses to males during the transition from virginity to maternity. Importantly, this increase reverses after the females become post-lactational, indicating that it is not simply due to accumulated GCaMP expression. In contrast, α cells do not exhibit such a dramatic change. These data support Model 3, among the 4 classes of cellular models that could in principle explain this behavioral switch (Figure 1B and 7M). The ability of optogenetic ß cell activation to suppress sexual receptivity in virgins further suggests that these cells may normally inhibit sexual receptivity in lactating females, where they are more active (Figure 7M).

Our observations raise the question of the neural and molecular mechanisms by which ß cells become more responsive to male cues in lactating females. In principle, the excitability of these neurons could increase, due to a loss of local inhibitory input or to changes in the intrinsic biophysical properties of these cells. Alternatively, there could be a state-dependent gating event "upstream" of ß cells, which increases the amount of excitatory input they receive from male-responsive neurons elsewhere in the circuit. Answering this question is an important subject for future investigation. The identification of hormonal or other factors that trigger these changes during pregnancy and/or parturition will be of interest as well.

In males, VMHvl^{Esr1} neuronal activity reflects both intruder sex and social behavior [74]. It has been difficult to separate functionally the encoding of these two features, because intruder sex and social behavior are tightly coupled in males [3,4,74]. In lactating females, by contrast, aggressiveness can be triggered by either male or female intruders. The fact that ß cells are comparably activated by males and females in lactating dams, but are more strongly activated in aggressive than in non-aggressive mothers (Figure 6 and S5), strongly suggests that these cells encode aggressiveness rather than simply intruder sex (although we cannot exclude the existence of sex-specific subsets of ß cells). By extension, the same may be true in males.

Sex specific cell types and functions

VMHvl is highly sexually dimorphic, with respect to gene expression and connectivity [29,56,75]. More recently, single-cell RNAseq has revealed that subsets of VMHvl*Esr1* neurons are male- or female-specific [61]. Here we assign a functional role to a female-specific cell type (Tsix_Esr1_2) in sexual receptivity. This is concordant with the fact that mating behavior is highly sexually dimorphic – lordosis is only performed by females and not by males.

In males, aggression activates both a dimorphic VMHvl*Esr1* cell type (Esr1_7) and a nondimorphic cell type (Esr1_4) [61]. In females, by contrast, only the non-dimorphic cell type is active during aggression. Similarly, in *Drosophila* there is evidence for a non-dimorphic aggression-promoting cell type, CAP, that may control an aggressive motive state (Chiu *et al.*, 2021). However, there are also dimorphic cell types that promote aggression in each sex. In females, the aggression-specific cell type pC1d (Deutsch *et al.*, 2020; Schretter *et al.*, 2020, Chiu *et al.,* 2021) is located in a cluster that also contains a closely related subtype, pC1a, which controls female sexual receptivity [78]. Thus, in both female mice and female flies, there is a close anatomic and genetic relationship between the neuronal subtypes that control sexual receptivity or aggression.

Figures

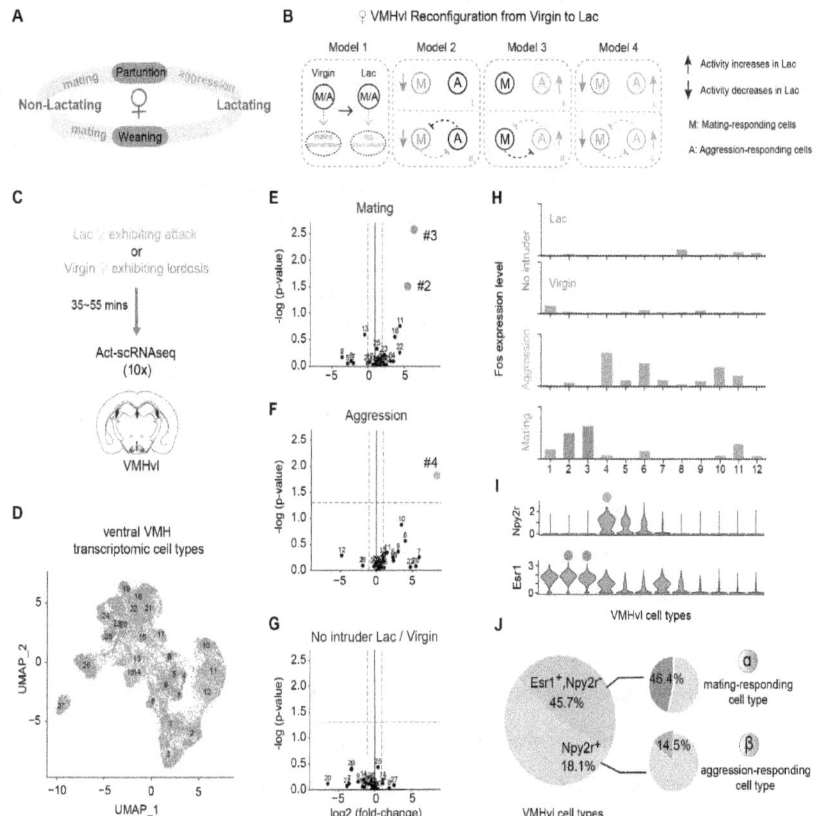

Figure 1. Distinct VMH transcriptomic cell types are activated during female mating and aggression.

(A)   Female mice adjust social behaviors according to their lactation cycle. The start of the lactating phase is always accompanied by a decrease in sexual behaviors and an onset of aggressive behaviors; at the end of the lactating phase, sexual behaviors resume, and aggression disappears.

(B)Potential cellular mechanisms underlying changes in female VMHvl^{Esr1} activity from the virgin to the lactating state. Model 1: The VMHvl^{Esr1} neurons controlling socio-sexual behavior are the same in virgin and lactating females, and critical changes occur at their downstream targets to promote mating (in virgins) or aggression (in lactating dams). (In a variant of Model 1 (not shown) different cells control mating vs. aggression, but their statedependent behavioral output is determined by changes in their downstream targets.) Models 2-4, distinct subsets VMHvl^{Esr1} cells control mating in virgins and aggression in lactating dams. Their relative activity differs depending on the animal's state and determines their behavioral output. The changes in lactating females could involve a decrease in the activity of mating neurons (Model 2); an increase in the activity of aggression neurons (Model 3); or both (Model 4). Models 2-4 can be further subdivided according to the presence (II) or absence (I) of reciprocal inhibitory interactions (likely indirect) between mating and aggression cells. Colored symbols indicate where the lactation-dependent changes occur. The change in the activity of these different subpopulations could reflect cell-intrinsic changes, or changes in input strength.

(C) Schematic of Act-seq protocol.

(D) UMAP plot color-coded by clusters identified in tissue dissected from female ventral VMH (N=19,103; 27 clusters).

(E-G) "Volcano plots" showing *Fos* expression levels in 27 VMH cell types from the following animals: (E) lactating females exhibiting attacks vs. control, (F) virgin females exhibiting lordosis vs. control, (G) control lactating females vs. control virgin females. Colored dots indicate cell types with *Fos* expression fold change >2 (x axis cut-off) and P <0.05 (y axis cut-off; gray dashed lines).

(H) *Fos* expression levels in 12 VMHvl cell types from control lactating females, control virgin females (No intruder), lactating females exhibiting attacks (Aggression) and virgin females exhibiting lordosis (Mating). Colored bars show T-types with statistically significant increases (fold change >2 & P <0.05) in *Fos* expression relative to no-intruder controls (see also Figure S2C).

(I) Violin plot illustrating expression levels of *Npy2r* and *Esr1* in 12 VMHvl cell types. (J) Summary of composition of VMHvl cell types. Left, shaded green: VMHvl$^{Esr1+,Npy2r-}$ cells; shaded yellow: VMHvl^{Npy2r+} cells; gray: VMHvl$^{Esr1-,Npy2r-}$ cells. Right, green: Percentage of mating-activated cell types (#2, #3), as detected by a significant and >2-fold increase in *Fos* expression, among VMHvl$^{Esr1+,Npy2r-}$ cells (a); orange: Percentage of aggression-activated cell type (#4) as detected by *Fos* expression among VMHvl^{Npy2r+} cells (b). *Fos* expression in VMHvl substantially underestimates the fraction of neurons active during a given behavior, as measured by electrophysiological recordings [28].

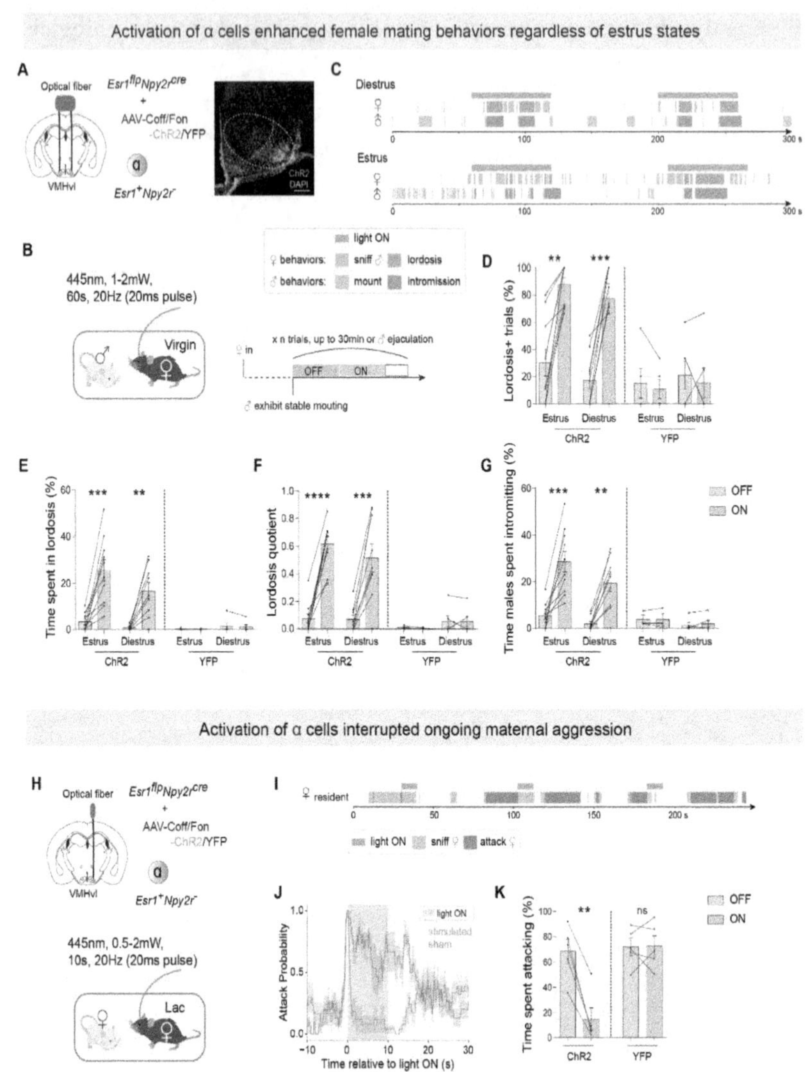

Figure 2. VMHvl α cells control female receptivity and inhibit maternal aggression.

(A) Left, strategy to activate VMHvl$^{Esr1+, Npy2r-}$ cells (α) in virgin females by optogenetics. Right, representative ChR2 expression in VMHvl α cells. Scalebar, 200um.

(B) Behavioral paradigm and illustration of stimulation scheme for one session (also see Methods).

(C)Representative raster plots illustrating light-induced behaviors in tested female and paired male.

(D)Fraction of trials where female exhibited lordosis,

(E) fraction of time female spent in lordosis,

(F) lordosis quotient (lordosis time/male mounting or intromission time),

(G)fraction of time males spent intromitting during light ON or light OFF periods, in estrus or diestrus intact (non-ovariectomized) ChR2/YFP-expressing females.

(H)Strategy to activate VMHvl$^{Esr1+,Npy2r-}$ cells (α) in lactating females by optogenetics. (I) Representative raster plots illustrating light-induced behaviors in aggressive lactating female.

(J)   Average attack probability. In blue, stimulated trials with light ON; in grey, sham trials with light OFF.

(K)   Fraction of time lactating female spent attacking during 10-second stimulated or sham periods.

*p<0.05; **p<0.01; ***p<0.001; ****p<0.0001. Mean ± SEM.

Inhibition of β cells interrupts ongoing maternal aggression

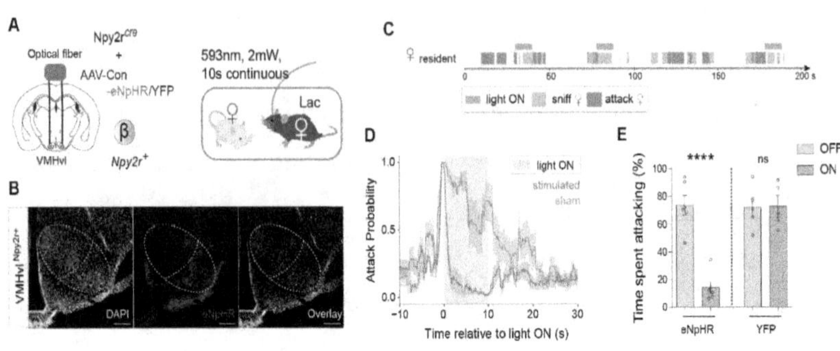

Activation of β cells is sufficient to evoke aggression in virgin females

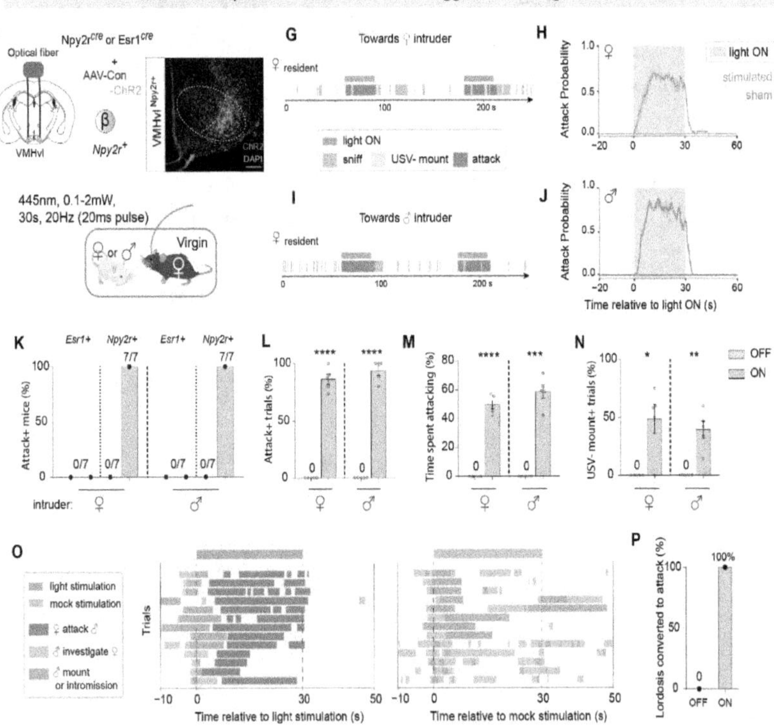

Figure 3. Activation of VMHvl ß cells evoked female aggression regardless of state.

(A)   Strategy to inhibit VMHvl^{Npy2r+} cells (β) in aggressive lactating females by optogenetics.

(B)Representative eNpHR expression in VMHvl β cells. Scalebar, 200um.

(C)Representative raster plots illustrating light-induced behaviors in aggressive lactating. (D) Average attack probability. In yellow, stimulated trials with light ON; in grey, sham trials with light OFF.

(E)   Fraction of time lactating female spent attacking during 10-second stimulated or sham stimulated periods.

(F)   Strategy to activate VMHvl^{Npy2r+} cells (β) or VMHvl^{Esr1+} cells in non-aggressive virgin females by optogenetics.

(G, I) Representative raster plots illustrating light-induced behaviors in virgin female towards (F) female or (H) male intruders.

(H, J) Average attack probability towards (G) female intruder and (I) male intruder. In blue, stimulated trials light ON; in grey, sham trials with light OFF.

(K)Fraction of mice for whom attack was induced by activating β or VMHvl^{Esr1+} cells.

(L) Fraction of trials with *Npy2r^{cre}* female exhibiting attack.

(M)   Fraction of time *Npy2r^{cre}* female exhibited attack during a trial.

(N)Fraction of trials with *Npy2r^{cre}* female exhibiting USV$^-$ mounting.

(O-P) Activation of β cells converted ongoing mating behaviors to attack in virgin females. (O) Behavior raster plot of individual trials. (P) Fraction of females exhibiting lordosis converted to attack.

*p<0.05, **p<0.01, ***p<0.001, ****p<0.0001. Mean ± SEM.

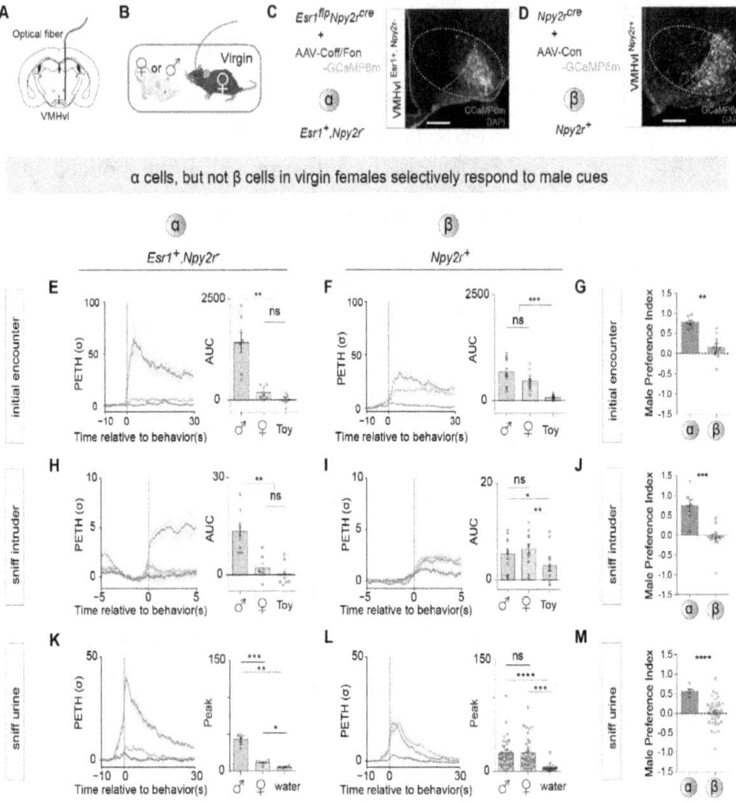

Figure 4. VMHvl α cells, but not ß cells in virgin females selectively respond to male cues.

A) Schematic illustrating fiber photometry recording in VMHvl.

(B) Schematic illustrating behavioral test of social interaction in virgin females.

(C-D) Representative GCaMP6m expression in (C) VMHvl α and (D) β cells. Scalebar, 200um.

(E-F) Left, Peri-event time histogram (PETH) (E) α cells or (F) β cells, aligned to initial encounter with intruders. Initial encounter occurred immediately after intruder introduction. Right, area under the curve (AUC) represents timespan 0 to 30 seconds after the initial encounter.

(G) Male Preference Index (MPI) of initial encounter from α and β cells. MPI = (AUC of initial encounter with male - AUC of initial encounter with female) / (AUC of initial encounter with male + AUC of initial encounter with female).

(H-I) Left, PETH from (H) α cells or (I) β cells, aligned to sniffing intruder; these are defined as sniffing bouts occurring > 1 minute after intruder introduction. Sniffing bouts followed by male mounting were excluded. Right, AUC represents timespan 0 to 3 seconds after sniffing intruder.

(J) MPI of sniffing intruder from α and β cells. MPI = (AUC sniffing male - AUC sniffing female) / (AUC sniffing male + AUC sniffing female).

(K-L) Left, PETH from (K) α and (L) β cells, aligned to first sniff of urine. Right, Peak PETH between time 0 to 10 seconds relative to first sniff of urine.

(M) MPI of first sniff of urine from α and β cells. MPI = (Peak of sniffing of male urine - Peak of sniffing of female urine) / (Peak of sniffing of male urine + Peak of sniffing of female urine).

**p<0.01; ***p<0.001; ****p<0.0001; ns, not significant. Mean ± SEM.

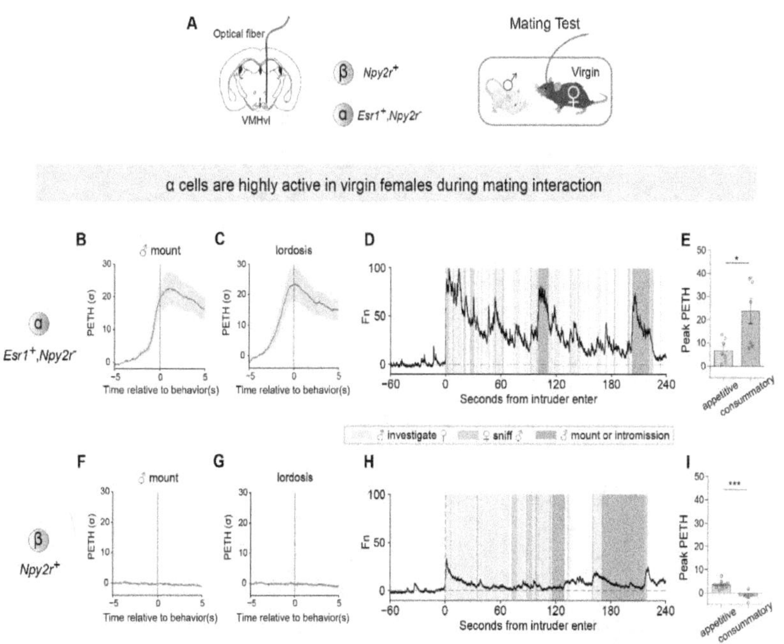

Figure 5. VMHvl α cells are highly active in virgin females during mating behaviors. (A) Schematic illustrating fiber photometry recording in VMHvl and behavioral test in virgin females.

(B-C) PETH of GCaMP6m fluorescence in α cells aligned to onset of (B) male mounting and (C) lordosis.

(F-G) PETH in β aligned to onset of (F) male mounting and (G) lordosis.

(D, H) Representative normalized calcium traces from (D) α cells and (H) β cells during mating interaction. Colored shading marks behavioral episodes.

(E, I) Peak of PETH from (E) α cells and (I) β cells aligned to onset of appetitive phase (sniff) or consummatory phase (male mounting or intromission) during mating interaction.

*p <0.05; ns, not significant. Mean ± SEM.

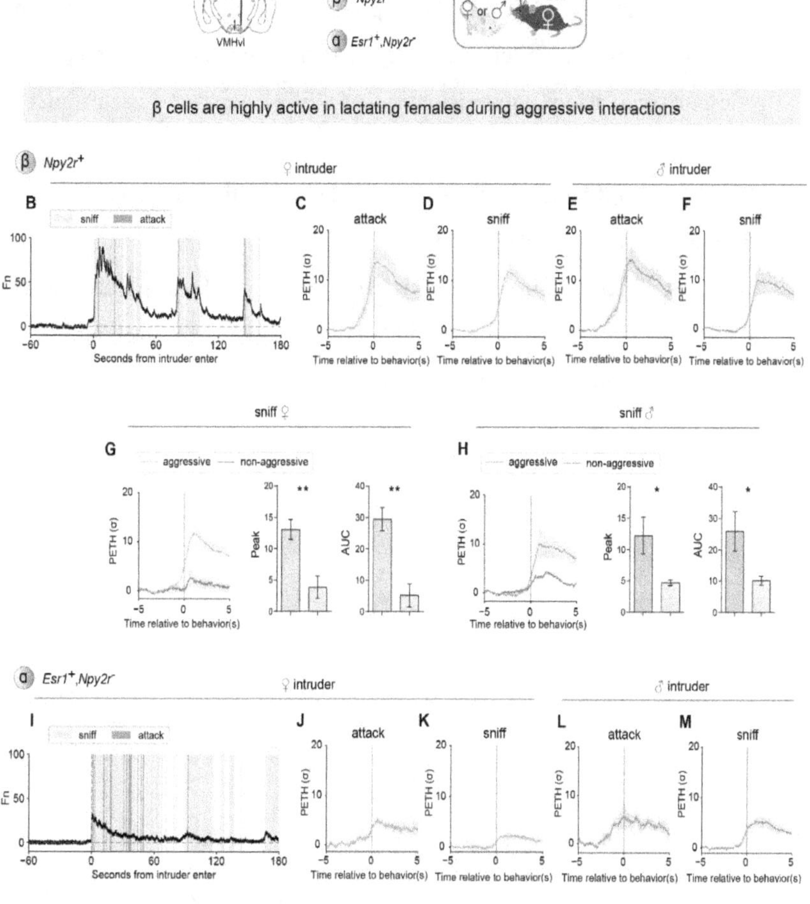

Figure 6. VMHvl β cells are highly active in lactating females during aggressive interactions.

(A) Schematic illustrating fiber photometry recording in VMHvl β cells and α cells, and behavioral test of aggressive behaviors in lactating females.

(B) Representative normalized GCaMP6m trace from β cells during aggressive interaction with female intruder. Colored shading marks behavioral episodes.

(C-F) PETH of β cell activity aligned to onset of (C) attack and (D) sniffing of female intruder, or (E) attack and (F) sniffing of male intruder. Sniffing includes all sniffs, whether or not followed by attack.

(G-H) β cell responses during sniffing of (G) female or (H) male intruders in aggressive (colored lines) vs. constitutively non-aggressive (gray lines) lactating females. Left, PETH of β cell activity aligned to onset of sniffing. Data from aggressive females is replicated from panels (D) and (F) to facilitate comparisons. Right, quantification of PETH peak and area under the curve (AUC).

(I) Representative normalized GCaMP6m trace from α cells during aggressive interaction with female intruder.

(J-M) PETH of α cell activity aligned to onset of (J) attack and (K) sniffing of female intruder, or (L) attack and (M) sniffing of male intruder.

*p<0.05; **p<0.01; ns, not significant. Mean ± SEM.

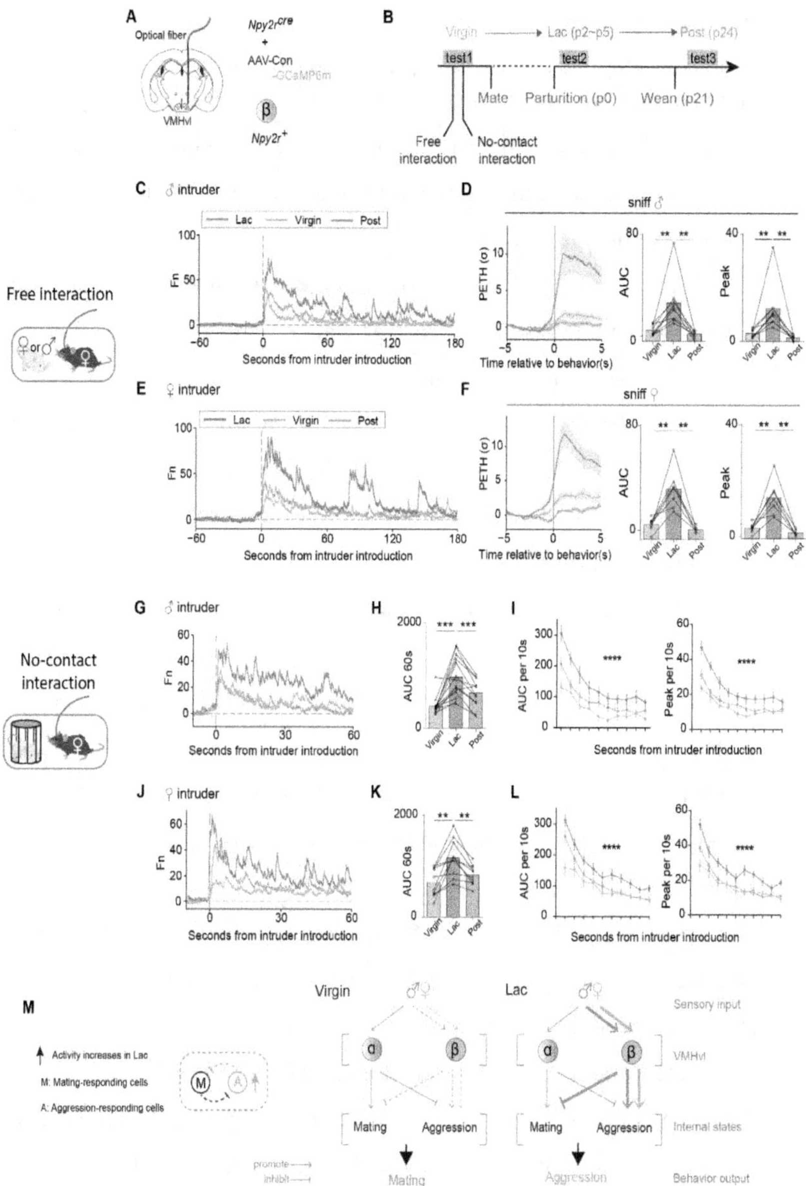

Figure 7. Neural response of VMHvl ß cells to social cues is lactation state dependent.

(A)Schematic illustrating fiber photometry recording in VMHvl β cells.

(B)Timeline of longitudinal behavioral tests and recordings in the same individuals across their lactation cycle. Each female was tested 3 times in the virgin, lactating (Lac) and postlactating (Post) phases. Parturition date was counted as p0.

(C, E) Representative examples of normalized GCaMP6m traces from the same individual female resident across her lactation cycle, during free interactions with (C) male or (E) female intruders.

(D, F) Left, PETHs from three phases of lactation cycle aligned to onset of sniffing of (D) male or (F) female. Right, quantification of PETH peak and AUC. No change of statistical significances after removing the highest data points in each group (see Supplemental Table 1).

(G, J) Representative of normalized GCaMP6m traces from the same individual female resident across lactation cycle during no-contact interaction with (G) male or (J) female intruder protected by an inverted pencil cup (schematic).

(H, K) AUC of neural activity recorded from three phases of lactation cycle during the first 60 seconds relative to introduction of pencil cup-protected (H) male or (K) female.

(I, L) Averaged AUC or peak of neural activity during each 10-second time bin relative to introduction of pencil cup-protected (I) male or (L) female, from the three phases of the lactation cycle.

(M) Left, Model 3 II, related to Figure 1B. Right, schematic illustrating the information flow during social interaction in virgin and lactating females: from sensory inputs to brain circuits to emotional states to behavioral output. Line thickness represents information strength.

Blue: male intruder; Pink: female intruder.

**p<0.01, ***p<0.001; Mean ± SEM.

Supplementary figures

Figure S1

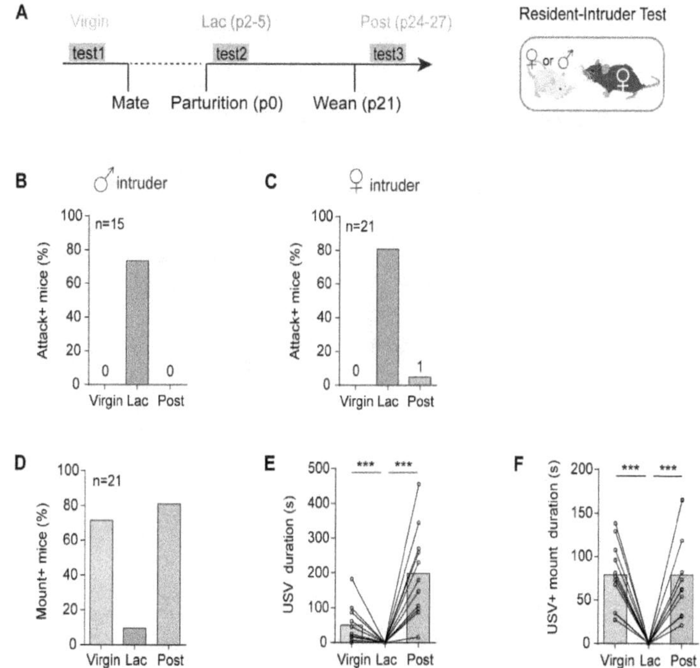

Related to Figure 1.

Figure S1. Reversible switch of social behaviors in C57BL/6N female mice.

(A) Timeline and schematic of longitudinal behavioral tests. Parturition date counted as p0. (B-C) Percentage of females exhibiting attack behavior towards (B) male intruder or (C) female intruder in virgin, lactating or post-lactating state.

(D) Percentage of females in virgin, lactating or post-lactating state exhibiting mounting behavior towards a female intruder.

(E-F) Duration of (E) ultrasonic vocalizations (USVs) emitted, or duration of (F) maletypical mounting behavior coupled with USVs by the same females, in the virgin, lactating and post-lactating states.

***p<0.001. Mean ± SEM.

Figure S2

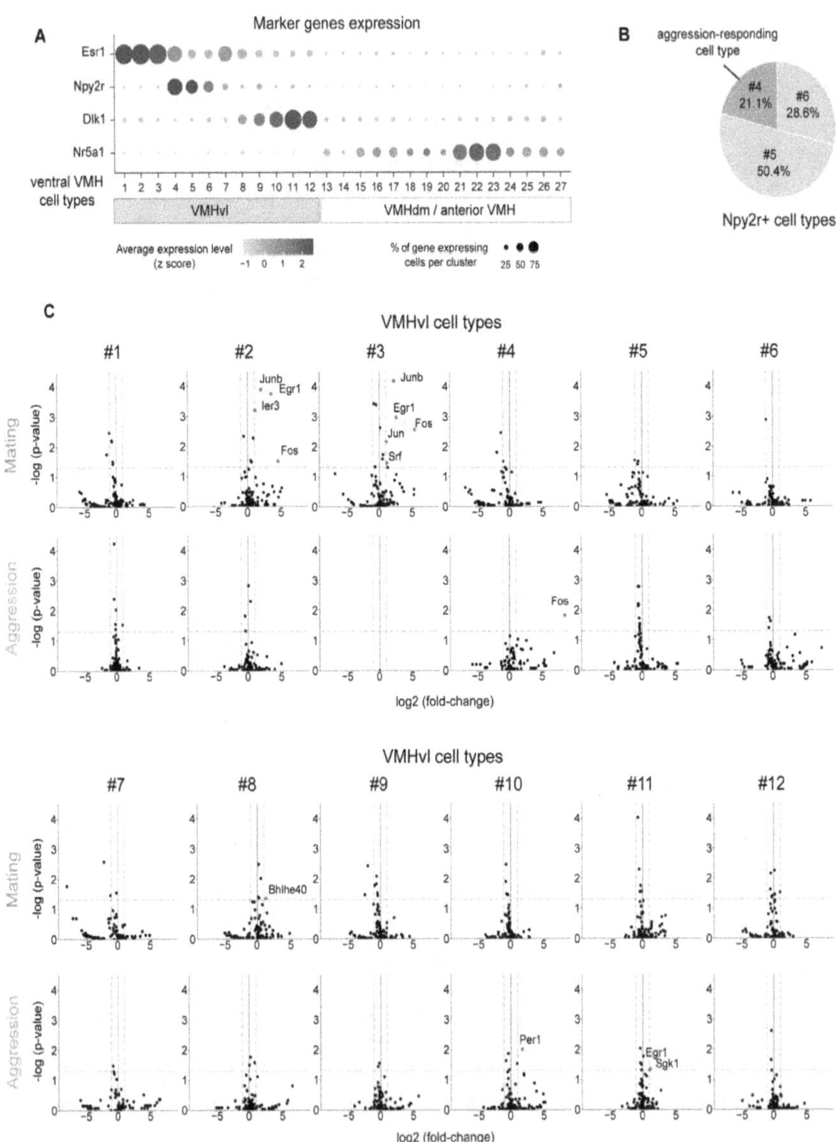

A

B

C

Related to Figure 1.

Figure S2. Additional information about female ventral VMH transcriptomic cell types.

(A)   Expression level of marker genes for VMHvl and VMHdm / anterior VMH in 27 female ventral VMH cell types.

(B)   Pie chart illustrating the percentage of different VMHvl transcriptomic cell types that express Npy2r. Only cluster #4 is activated (IEG induction) during aggression (orange sector).

(C)   "Volcano plots" showing expression levels of all 139 IEGs in 12 VMHvl cell types from the following animals: lactating females exhibiting attacks vs. control, virgin females exhibiting lordosis vs. control. Colored dots indicate genes with expression fold change >2

(x axis cut-off) and P <0.05 (y axis cut-off; gray dashed lines).

Figure S3

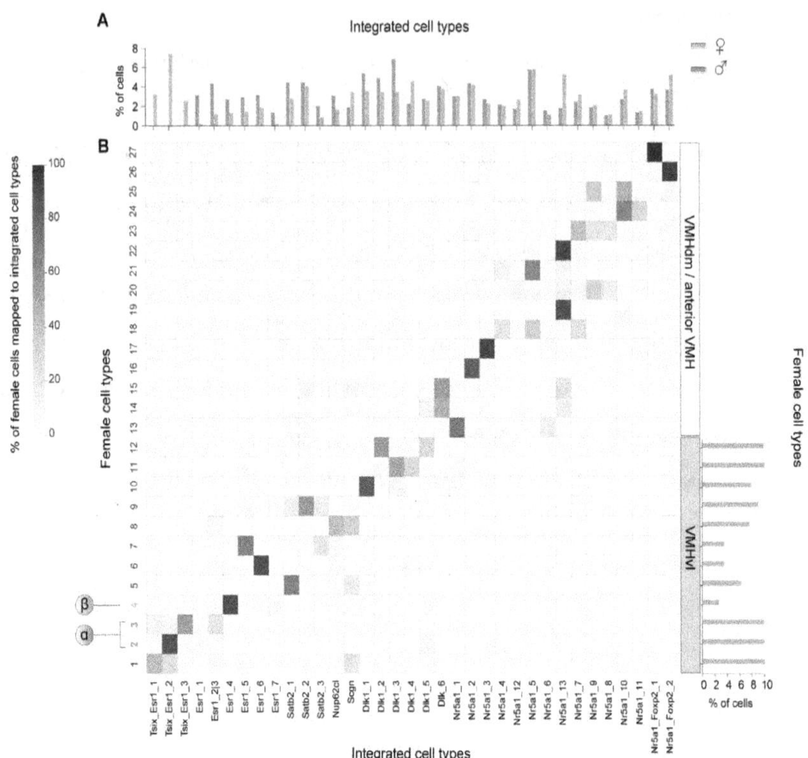

Related to Figure 1.

Figure S3. Comparison between male and female ventral VMH transcriptomes. (A) Cell number distributions of female (pink) and male (blue) integrated cell types in ventral VMH (previous published data-guided integration [61]).

(B) Left, percentage of female cells (from this study) mapped to integrated VMH cell types. Right, cell number distributions of female cells (from this study) in VMHvl. α: female mating-responding cells; β: female aggression-responding cells.

Figure S4

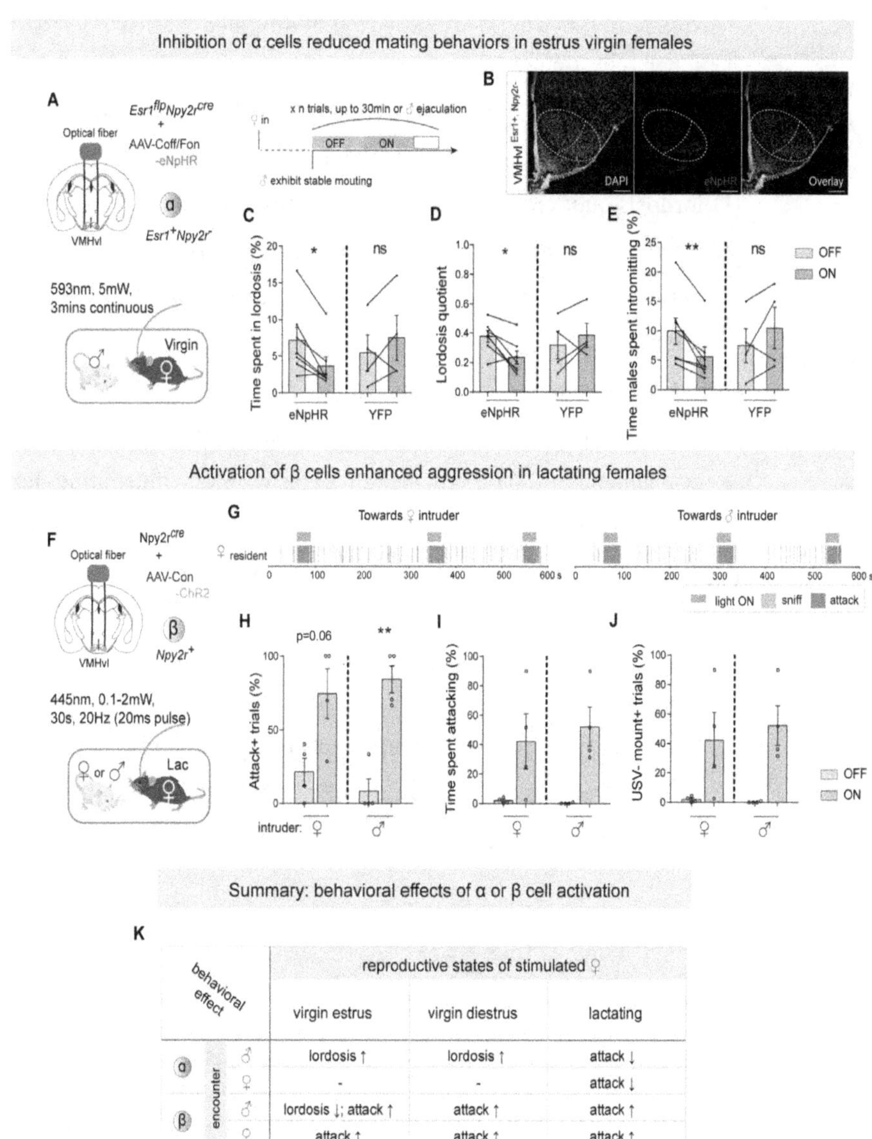

Related to Figure 2 and 3.

Figure S4. Additional information for optogenetic perturbations for VMHvl α and β cells.

(A-E) Inhibition of α cells reduced mating behaviors in estrus virgin females.

(A) Strategy to inhibit VMHvl$^{Esr1+,Npy2r-}$ cells (α) in virgin females by optogenetics and behavioral paradigm and illustration of stimulation scheme for one session.

(B) Representative eNpHR expression in VMHvl α cells. Scalebar, 200um.

(C) Fraction of time female spent in lordosis,

(D) lordosis quotient (lordosis time/male mounting or intromission time),

(E) fraction of time males spent intromitting during light ON or light OFF periods, in estrus intact (non-ovariectomized) ChR2/YFP-expressing females.

(F-I) Activation of β cells enhanced aggression in lactating females.

(F) Strategy to activate VMHvl^{Npy2r+} cells (β) in lactating females by optogenetics. (G) Representative raster plots illustrating light-induced behaviors in lactating female towards female or male intruders.

(H) Fraction of trials where lactating female exhibited attack behavior.

(I) Fraction of time lactating female spent attacking during a trial.

(J) Fraction of trials where lactating females exhibited USV$^-$ mounting behavior.

(K) Summary table for behavioral effects of α or β cell activation in females at different reproductive states. ↑evoke or enhance; ↓inhibit.

*$p<0.05$; **$p<0.01$; Mean ± SEM.

Figure S5

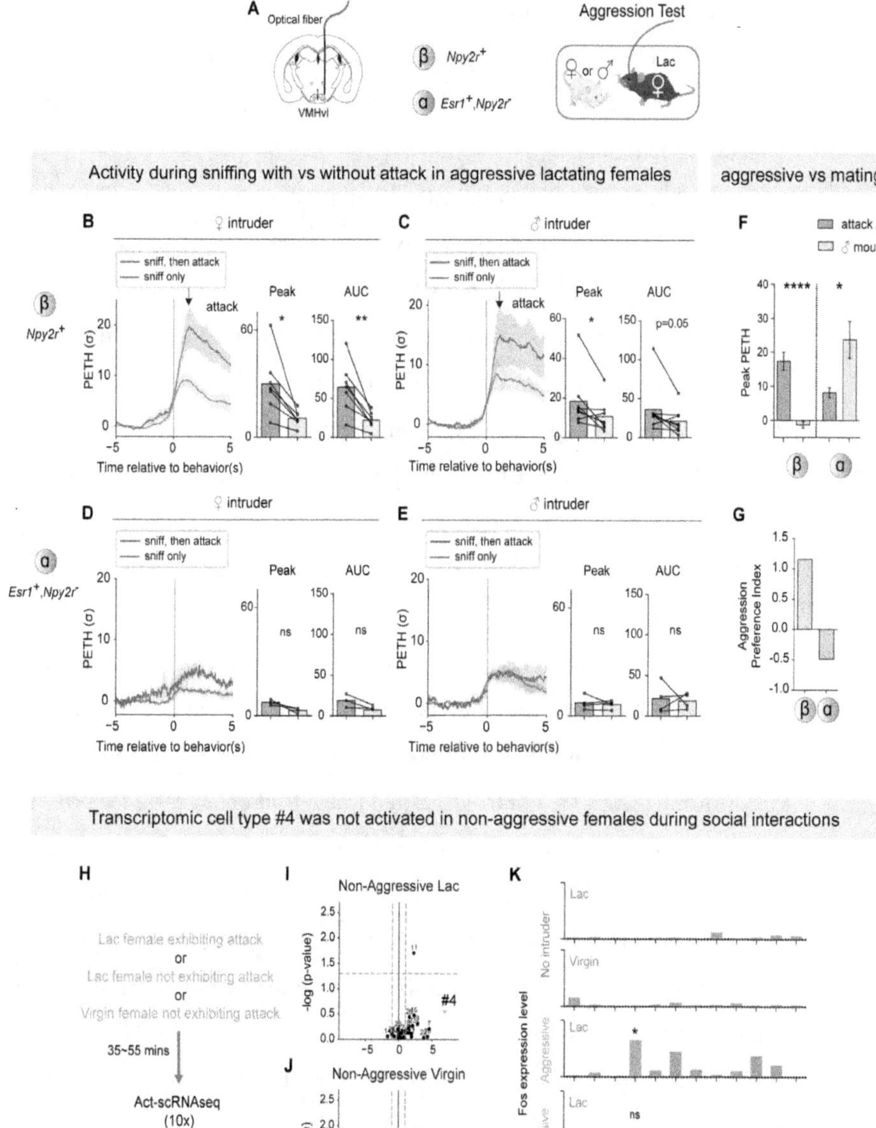

Related to Figure 6.

Figure S5. VMHvl β cells are highly active in lactating females during aggressive interactions.

(A) Left, schematic illustrating fiber photometry recording in VMHvl β and α cells. Right, schematic illustrating behavioral test of aggressive behaviors in lactating females.

(B-C) Left, PETH of β cells activity aligned to onset of sniffing of (B) female or (C) male followed or not followed by attack. Right, quantification of PETH peak and area under the curve (AUC).

(D-E) Left, PETH of α cells activity aligned to onset of sniffing of (D) female or (E) male followed or not followed by attack.

(F-G) Comparison of neural responses during aggression vs. mating behaviors. (F) PETH peak levels of VMHvl β and α cell activity at consummatory phase during aggressive or mating interactions with male intruder. (G) Aggression preference index = Peak PETH at (attack − mounted) / (attack + mounted).

(H-K) Act-seq results from aggressive vs. non-aggressive females following social interactions with female intruders. (H) Schematic of Act-seq protocol. (I-J) "Volcano plots" showing Fos expression levels in 27 VMH cell types from (I) lactating females not exhibiting attacks vs. control, (J) virgin females not exhibiting attack vs. control. Dashed lines: fold change = 2 (x axis cut-off) and $P = 0.05$ (y axis cut-off). (K) *Fos* expression levels in 12 VMHvl cell types from control lactating females, control virgin females (No intruder), lactating females exhibiting attacks (Aggressive), lactating and virgin females not exhibiting attack (Non-Aggressive). Orange colored: aggression-responding cluster #4 (See Figure 1F).

*p<0. 05; **p<0.01; ***p<0.001; ****p<0.0001; ns, no significance. Mean ± SEM.

Figure S6

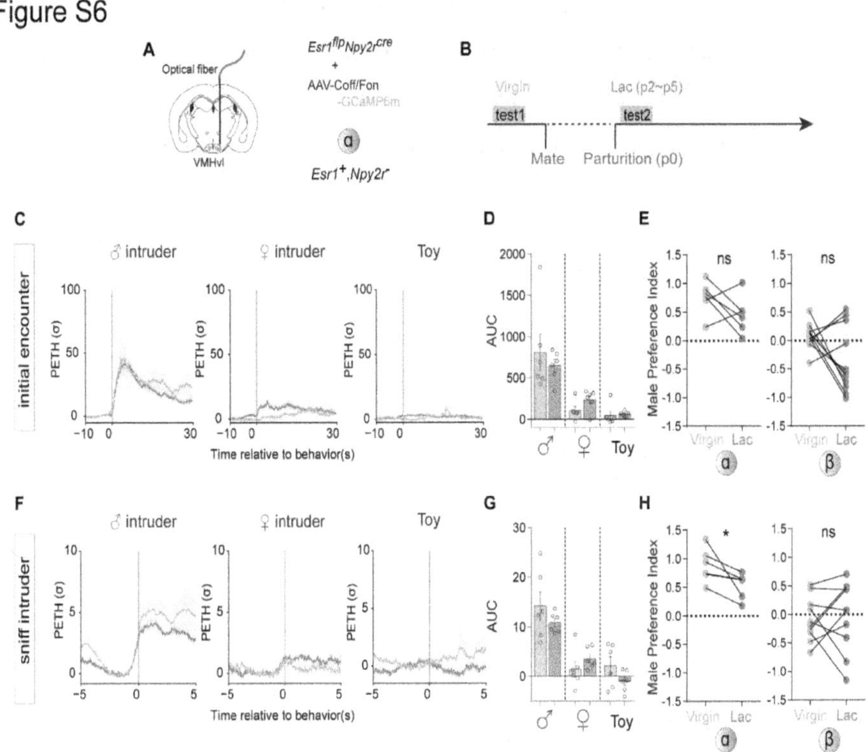

Related to Figure 7.

Figure S6. Activity of VMHvl α cells in social interaction is not state-dependent.

(A) Schematic illustrating fiber photometry recording of VMHvl α cells.

(B) Timeline representing the conducting of longitudinal behavioral tests and recording in the same individuals in virgin and lactating states. Parturition date was counted as p0. (C) PETH of α cell activity in virgin and lactating state aligned to onset of initial encounters with male, female and toy.

(D) AUC represents timespan 0-30 seconds after initial encounters.

(E) Within-subject comparison of male preference index (MPI) between virgin and lactating state from α and β. MPI = AUC of initial encounter with (male – female) / (male + female). (F) PETH of α cell activity in virgin and lactating state aligned to onset of sniffing of male, female and toy.

(G) AUC represents timespan 0-3 seconds after sniffing of intruders.

(H)Within-subject comparison of male preference index (MPI) between virgin and lactating state from α and β cells. MPI = AUC of sniffing of (male − female) / (male + female).

*p<0.05; ns, no significance. Mean ± SEM.

Figure S7

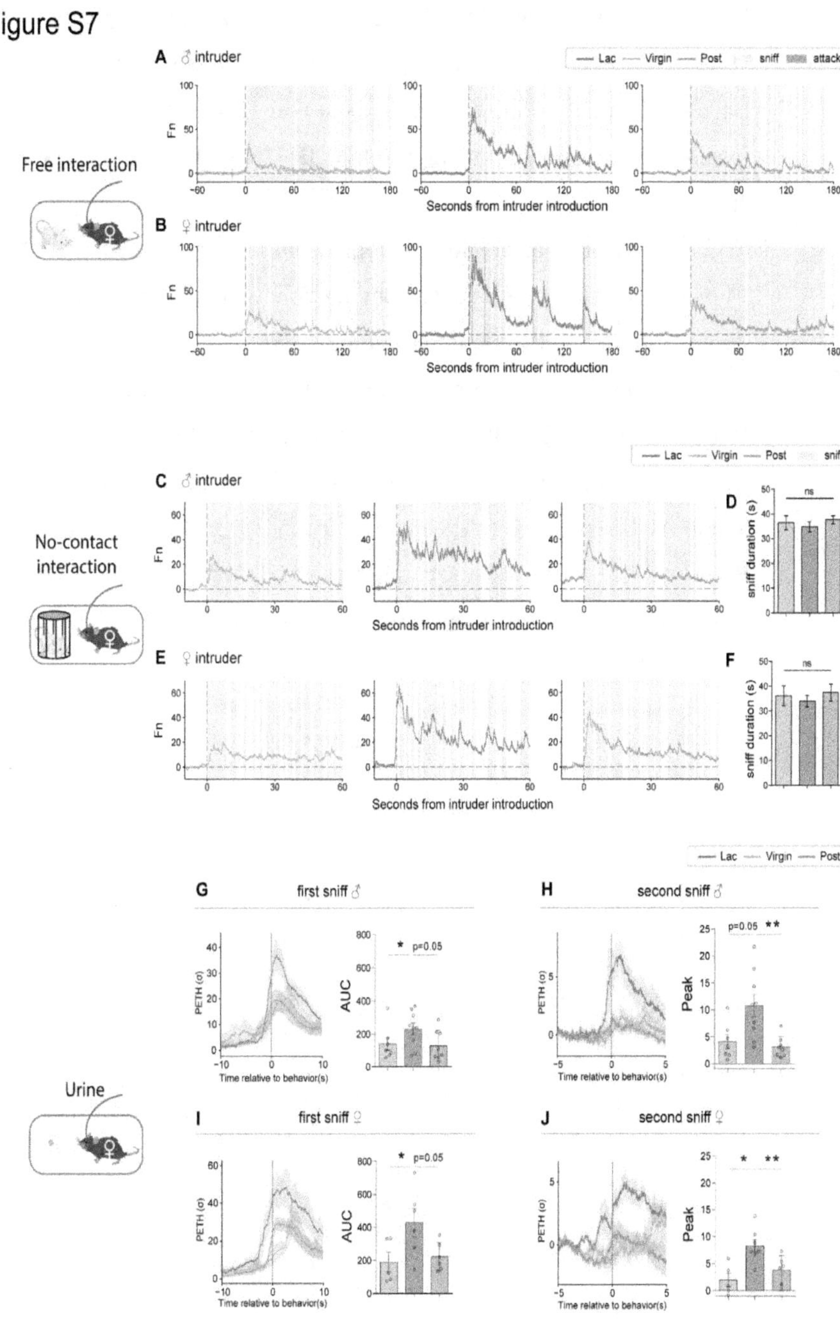

Related to Figure 7.

Figure S7. Response of VMHvl β cells to social cues depends on lactation state. (A-B) Behavioral raster plots of representative normalized GCaMP6m trace from β cells during free-interaction with (A) male intruder and (B) female intruder. Corresponding to Figure S7C,E. Colored shading marks behavioral episodes.

(C,E) Behavioral raster plots of representative normalized GCaMP6m trace from β cells during no-contact-interaction with (C) male intruder and (E) female intruder. Corresponding to Figure S7G,J.

(D,F) Total sniff duration in the first minute of no-contact interaction in three lactation states. (G-J) β cell responses to urine in three lactation states. (G,I) Left, PETH of β cells activity at first sniff of (G) male urine or (I) female urine. Right, AUC represents timespan 0-10 seconds from behavior onset. (H,J) Left, PETH of β cell activity at second sniff of (H) female urine or (J) male urine. Right, AUC represents timespan 0-3 seconds from behavior onset.

*$p<0.05$; **$p<0.01$. Mean ± SEM.

Supplemental Table 1

Related to STAR Methods section QUANTIFICATION AND STATISTICAL ANALYSIS.

Panel	Comparison	Test	p-value	N
1E	Lac attack vs Lac control	Wilcoxon Rank Sum	\	\
1F	Virgin lordosis vs Virgin control	Wilcoxon Rank Sum	\	\
1G	Virgin control vs Lac control	Wilcoxon Rank Sum	\	\
2D	ON vs OFF, Estrus	Wilcoxon Rank Sum	0.002	10
2D	ON vs OFF, Diestrus	Paired t test	0.0005	9
2E	ON vs OFF, Estrus	Paired t test	0.0006	10
2E	ON vs OFF, Diestrus	Wilcoxon Rank Sum	0.0078	9
2F	ON vs OFF, Estrus	Paired t test	<0.0001	10
2F	ON vs OFF, Diestrus	Paired t test	0.0007	9
2G	ON vs OFF, Estrus	Paired t test	0.0006	10
2G	ON vs OFF, Diestrus	Wilcoxon Rank Sum	0.0078	9
2K	ON vs OFF	Paired t test	0.0021	5
2K	ON vs OFF, YFP	Paired t test	0.9204	5
3E	ON vs OFF	Paired t test	<0.0001	6
3E	ON vs OFF, YFP	Paired t test	0.9123	5
3L	ON vs OFF, Female	Paired t test	<0.0001	5
3L	ON vs OFF, Male	Paired t test	<0.0001	5
3M	ON vs OFF, Female	Paired t test	<0.0001	5
3M	ON vs OFF, Male	Paired t test	0.0002	5
3N	ON vs OFF, Female	Paired t test	0.0192	5
3N	ON vs OFF, Male	Paired t test	0.0067	5
4E	Male vs Female	Paired t test	0.0027	8
4E	Male vs Toy	Wilcoxon Rank Sum	0.0078	8
4E	Female vs Toy	Wilcoxon Rank Sum	0.0781	8
4H	Male vs Female	Paired t test	0.0025	8
4H	Male vs Toy	Paired t test	0.0013	8
4H	Female vs Toy	Paired t test	0.9927	8
4K	Male vs Female	Paired t test	0.0004	6
4K	Male vs water	Mann-Whitney U	0.0095	6,5
4K	Female vs water	Mann-Whitney U	0.019	6,5
4L	Male vs Female	Wilcoxon Rank Sum	0.7402	35
4L	Male vs water	Mann-Whitney U	<0.0001	35,19
4L	Female vs water	Mann-Whitney U	<0.0001	35,19
4F	Male vs Female	Wilcoxon Rank Sum	0.0537	11
4F	Male vs Toy	Paired t test	0.0001	11
4F	Female vs Toy	Paired t test	0.0002	11
4I	Male vs Female	Paired t test	0.8065	8
4I	Male vs Toy	Paired t test	0.0414	8
4I	Female vs Toy	Paired t test	0.0026	8
4G	alpha vs beta	Mann-Whitney U	0.0018	8,11
4J	alpha vs beta	Mann-Whitney U	0.0003	8
4M	alpha vs beta	Welch-corrected t test	<0.0001	6,35
5E	appetitve vs consummatory	Unpaired t test	0.0119	7
5I	appetitve vs consummatory	Unpaired t test	0.0002	11,5
6G	AGG vs non-AGG	Mann-Whitney U	0.0033	14,5

Panel	Comparison	Test	p-value	N
7F	Virgin vs Lac(highest value removed)	Paired t test	0.002	6
7F	Post vs Lac, AUC	Paired t test	0.0035	6
7F	Post vs Lac(highest value removed)	Paired t test	0.0026	5
7K	Virgin vs Lac	Paired t test	0.0018	10
7K	Post vs Lac	Paired t test	0.0019	10
7H	Virgin vs Lac	Wilcoxon Rank Sum	0.0002	14
7H	Post vs Lac	Paired t test	0.0002	12
7I	Virgin vs Lac, AUC	Two-way ANOVA	<0.0001	10
7I	Post vs Lac, AUC	Two-way ANOVA	<0.0001	10
7I	Virgin vs Lac, peak	Two-way ANOVA	<0.0001	10
7I	Post vs Lac, peak	Two-way ANOVA	<0.0001	10
7L	Virgin vs Lac, AUC	Two-way ANOVA	<0.0001	10
7L	Post vs Lac, AUC	Two-way ANOVA	<0.0001	10
7L	Virgin vs Lac, peak	Two-way ANOVA	<0.0001	10
7L	Post vs Lac, peak	Two-way ANOVA	<0.0001	10
S1E	Virgin vs Lac	Wilcoxon Rank Sum	0.001	11
S1E	Post vs Lac	Wilcoxon Rank Sum	0.001	11
S1F	Virgin vs Lac	Wilcoxon Rank Sum	0.001	11
S1F	Post vs Lac	Wilcoxon Rank Sum	0.001	11
S2C	Lac attack vs Lac control	Wilcoxon Rank Sum	\	\
S2C	Virgin lordosis vs Virgin control	Wilcoxon Rank Sum	\	\
S4C	ON vs OFF, eNpHR	Wilcoxon Rank Sum	0.0313	7
S4C	ON vs OFF, YFP	Wilcoxon Rank Sum	0.375	4
S4D	ON vs OFF, eNpHR	Paired t test	0.0155	7
S4D	ON vs OFF, YFP	Wilcoxon Rank Sum	0.625	4
S4E	ON vs OFF, eNpHR	Paired t test	0.007	7
S4E	ON vs OFF, YFP	Wilcoxon Rank Sum	0.5	4
S4H	Female	Paired t test	0.0656	4
S4H	Male	Paired t test	0.0025	4
S4I	Female	Paired t test	0.1237	4
S4I	Male	Paired t test	0.0282	4
S4J	Female	Paired t test	0.4226	3
S4J	Male	Paired t test	0.3061	4
S5B	Peak	Paired t test	0.0129	7
S5B	AUC	Paired t test	0.0048	7
S5C	Peak	Wilcoxon Rank Sum	0.0391	8
S5C	AUC	Wilcoxon Rank Sum	0.0547	8
S5D	Peak	Wilcoxon Rank Sum	0.25	4
S5D	AUC	Wilcoxon Rank Sum	0.25	4
S5E	Peak	Wilcoxon Rank Sum	>0.9999	4
S5E	AUC	Wilcoxon Rank Sum	0.875	4
S5F	Beta	Welch-corrected t test	<0.0001	9,5
S5F	Alpha	Welch-corrected t test	0.0284	4,7
S6D	Male	Paired t test	0.3224	6
S6D	Female	Paired t test	0.208	6

Panel	Comparison	Test	p-value	n	Panel	Comparison	Test	p-value	n
6G	AGG vs non-AGG	Mann-Whitney U	0.0012	14,5	S6D	Toy	Paired t test	0.1508	6
6H	AGG vs non-AGG	Mann-Whitney U	0.0112	9,4	S6E	Alpha	Paired t test	0.1747	6
6H	AGG vs non-AGG	Mann-Whitney U	0.0196	9,4	S6E	Beta	Paired t test	0.0609	11
7D	Virgin vs Lac, peak	Wilcoxon Rank Sum	0.0039	9	S6G	Male	Paired t test	0.554	6
7D	Virgin vs Lac(highest value removed)	Paired t test	0.0002	8	S6G	Female	Wilcoxon Rank Sum	0.1563	6
7D	Post vs Lac, peak	Wilcoxon Rank Sum	0.0078	8	S6G	Toy	Wilcoxon Rank Sum	0.4375	6
7D	Post vs Lac(highest value removed)	Paired t test	0.0004	7	S6H	Alpha	Wilcoxon Rank Sum	0.0313	6
7D	Virgin vs Lac, AUC	Wilcoxon Rank Sum	0.0039	9	S6H	Beta	Paired t test	0.8165	10
7D	Virgin vs Lac(highest value removed)	Paired t test	0.0004	8	S7G	Virgin vs Lac	Paired t test	0.015	4
7D	Post vs Lac, AUC	Wilcoxon Rank Sum	0.0078	8	S7G	Post vs Lac	Paired t test	0.0522	6
7D	Post vs Lac(highest value removed)	Paired t test	0.0014	7	S7H	Virgin vs Lac	Paired t test	0.0198	5
7F	Virgin vs Lac, peak	Paired t test	0.0057	7	S7H	Post vs Lac	Paired t test	0.0022	6
7F	Virgin vs Lac(highest value removed)	Paired t test	0.0037	6	S7I	Virgin vs Lac	Paired t test	0.028	7
7F	Post vs Lac, peak	Paired t test	0.0024	6	S7I	Post vs Lac	Paired t test	0.0524	8
7F	Post vs Lac(highest value removed)	Paired t test	0.0025	5	S7J	Virgin vs Lac	Paired t test	0.0515	7
7F	Virgin vs Lac, AUC	Paired t test	0.0051	7	S7J	Post vs Lac	Paired t test	0.0036	8

Materials and methods

EXPERIMENTAL MODEL AND SUBJECT DETAILS

Mice

All experimental procedures involving the use of live mice or their tissues were carried out in accordance with NIH guidelines and approved by the Institute Animal Care and Use Committee (IACUC) and the Institute Biosafety Committee (IBC) at the California Institute of Technology (Caltech). All mice in this study, including wild-type and transgenic mice, were bred at Caltech. Single-housed C57BL/6N female mice (2-5 months) were used as experimental mice. Group-housed sexually naïve BALB/c male and female mice (6~8 weeks) were used as intruder mice for resident-intruder test (see resident-intruder test section below), unless specifically indicated in the text. Single-housed, sexually experienced C57BL/6N male mice were used for the mating test (see mating test section below). *Npy2r^{cre}* mice (Jackson Laboratory stock no. 029285) (=N1), *Esr1^{cre}* mice, *Esr1^{flp}* mice (>N10) were backcrossed into the C57BL/6N background and bred at Caltech. Heterozygous *Npy2r^{cre}*, *Esr1^{cre}* or double heterozygote *Esr1^{flp/+}Npy2r^{cre/+}* mice were used for cell-specific targeting experiments and were genotyped by PCR analysis using genomic DNA from tail tissue. All mice were housed in ventilated micro-isolator cages in a temperature-controlled environment (median temperature 23°C, humidity 60%), under a reversed 11-h dark–13-h light cycle, with ad libitum access to food and water. Mouse cages were changed weekly. For the animals used for longitudinal tests across the lactation cycle, virgin females aged 8~10 weeks were singly housed for at least 3 days before conducting behavioral tests or mating. Once the pregnancy was visible, the male mouse was removed from the female's home cage. The first day pups were found was counted as postpartum day 0 (p0). Behavioral tests in the lactating state were conducted on p2 to p5. Pups were euthanized after p7. The natural lactation period for mice is 21 days; behavior tests in the post-lactation state were therefore conducted on p24 to p27.

Viruses

The following AAVs were used in this study, with injection titers as indicated. Viruses with a high original titer were diluted with clean PBS on the day of use. AAV2-EF1a-DIOhChR2(H134R)-EYFP (4 x e12 genome copies per ml), AAV5-EF1a-DIO-eNpHR3EYFP (4.5 x e12), AAV5-EF1a-DIO-YFP (6.5 x e12), AAV-DJ-hSyn-Coff/FonhChR2(H134R)-EYFP (4 x e12), and AAV-DJ-Syn-Coff/Fon-EYFP (3.4 x e12) were purchased from the UNC vector core. AAV1-Syn-Flex-GCaMP6m (2.1 x e13) and AAV8nEF-Coff/Fon-eNpHR3.3-EYFP (5.6 x e12) were purchased from Addgene. AAV-DJ-EF1aCoff/Fon-GCaMP6m (4.5 x e12, Addgene plasmid) was packaged at the HHMI Janelia Research Campus virus facility. "Con" indicates Cre-ON virus; "Coff/Fon" indicates Cre-OFF/FLP-ON virus.

METHOD DETAILS

Behavior tests

All behavioral experiments were performed in the animals' housing cages under red lighting during the animals' subjective night phase, using the previously described behavior recording setup [79]. Both top and front views of the behavior were filmed at 30 Hz using video recording software, StreamPix7 (Norpix). Audio recordings were collected at a 300-kHz sampling rate using an Avisoft-UltraSoundGate 116H kit with a condenser ultrasound CM16/CMPA microphone (Avisoft-Bioacoustics), positioned 45 cm above the arena. The audio and video recordings were synchronized to begin at the same time via a signal generated by StreamPix7. Mouse cages were not cleaned for a minimum of one day before the behavioral test, to retain the odors of the resident mouse. Behavior tests were performed during the subjective dark period of the mouse housing room day–night cycle. *Resident-intruder test* Sexually naïve group-housed Balb/c mice were used as intruders. On the test day, the tested female was introduced to the behavior recording setup in her home cage and allowed to rest for at least five minutes. For lactating females, pups were removed from cage before starting acclimation. Then a freely moving or pencil cup-confined male or female or was introduced to the tested female cage. The animals were allowed to interact freely for 3-30 minutes, as described in the text. An experimenter interrupted the interaction between animals if excessive aggression or male ejaculation were observed.

Mating test

For optogenetic experiments investigating α cell function in mating (Figure 2A-G and S4A-E and K), to acquire the maximum sexual activity in male during the limited time window for behavior test, single-housed and sexually experienced C57BL/6N male mice were used as resident and sexually primed before test. On the test day, a male was introduced to the behavior recording setup in his home cage and allowed to rest for at least five minutes. A random female was introduced to male cage and allowed to freely interact with the male mouse. When three male mounting attempts were observed, the random female was removed from male cage. Then the sexually primed male and the tested female were allowed to rest in the testing room for at least five minutes before starting behavior tests. The tested female was then introduced to the male cage. The animals were allowed to interact freely for up to 30 minutes. An experimenter interrupted the interaction between the animals if ejaculation was observed.

Urine presentation

For urine presentation experiments (Figure 4K-M and S7G-J), subject female mice were moved to a new cage one day before the experiment. Group-housed Balb/c female or male mice were used as urine donors. Immediately before testing, the donor mouse was lifted by the cervical region and the genital area was gently wiped with the top part of a Q-tip to absorb urine seeping from the anogenital region. The urine-soaked Q-tip was placed in the cage for two minutes, far away from the current location of the resident female, and then removed from the cage. Female and male urine samples were shuffled and presented to each female subject mouse two to three times, with at least a two-minute interval between presentations.
Urine from different donors was used every time.

Single-cell isolation and library construction
On the test day, female subjects were conducted a 15-minute resident-intruder test. A grouphoused Balb/c female were used as intruders to induce attack in subject lactating females, while a single-housed, sexually primed Balb/c male was used as resident to induce lordosis in subject virgin females. After the social interactions, the Balb/c mice were taken out of the cage, and the female subjects were left in the cage for 35-55 minutes. Lactating females exhibiting attack, virgin females exhibiting lordosis during the interaction, or control (no intruders) females were then collected immediately. We isolated single cells from the mouse brain as previously described [63], with some modifications. Subject females (4 brains collected at a time) were anaesthetized with isoflurane and transcardially perfused with cold NMDG-ACSF (adjusted to pH 7.3–7.4) containing CaCl2 (0.5 mM), glucose (25 mM), HCl (92 mM), HEPES (20 mM), KCl (2.5 mM), kynurenic acid (1 mM), MgSO4 (10 mM), NaHCO3 (30 mM), NaH2PO4 (1.2 mM), NMDG (92 mM), sodium L-ascorbate (5 mM),

sodium pyruvate (3 mM), and thiourea (2 mM), bubbled with carbogen gas. The brain was sectioned at 350 mm using vibratome (VT1000S, Leica Microsystems) on ice, and the regions of interest were microdissected under a dissecting microscope from two consecutive sections (-1.22 to -1.94 from Bregma (Franklin and Paxinos, 2008)). The microdissected tissues were collected in a microcentrifuge tube containing NMDG-ACSF with 30 mM actinomycin D on ice to suppress further immediate early gene (IEGs) activation [63]. Thereafter, the sections were transferred to a new microcentrifuge tube for papain digestion

(60 U/mL, Sigma, P3125-250MG; pre-activated at 34°C for 30 min) in Trehalose-HEPESACSF (adjusted to pH 7.3–7.4) containing actinomycin D (15mM), CaCl2 (2 mM), Lcysteine (2.5 mM), EDTA (0.5mM), glucose (25 mM), HEPES (20 mM), KCl (2.5 mM), kynurenic acid (1 mM), MgSO4 (2 mM), NaCl (92 mM), NaHCO3 (30 mM), NaH2PO4 (1.2 mM), trehalose (2.5% w/v). During incubation for enzymatic digestion (30 minutes at room temperature), the solution was gently mixed a few times every 5-10 minutes. After incubation, this solution was replaced with cold Trehalose-HEPES-ACSF containing Egg White/BSA ovomucoid inhibitor (3 mg/ mL, Worthington, OI-BSA) and DNase I (25 U/mL, Thermo scientific, 90083). The tissue pieces were dissociated into single cells by gentle, successive trituration through 300-mm and 150-mm Pasteur pipettes with polished tip openings. After trituration and filtering through a 40 mm cell strainer, single cells were pelleted at 300 g for 5 minutes at 4°C , and the supernatant was carefully removed; the cells were resuspended with cold Trehalose-HEPES-ACSF and filtered through a 20 mm filter. Cells were pelleted again at 300 g for 5 minutes at 4°C and resuspended with ResuspensionHEPES-ACSF containing BSA (0.05%), CaCl2 (2 mM), glucose (25 mM), HEPES (20 mM), KCl (2.5 mM), kynurenic acid (1 mM), MgSO4 (1 mM), NaCl (117 mM), NaHCO3 (30 mM), NaH2PO4 (1.2 mM) (osmolarity verified to be within 10 mOsm of TrehaloseHEPES-ACSF). After manually determining the cell concentration using a hemocytometer, suspensions were further diluted to desired concentrations (600–1,000 cells/mL) if necessary. The appropriate volume of

reverse transcription (RT) mix was added to target 10,000 cells recovered and loaded into the chip. Chromium Next GEM Single Cell 3′ GEM, Library & Gel Bead Kit v3.1 (PN-1000121), Chromium Next GEM Chip G Single Cell Kit (PN-1000120), and Chromium i7 Multiplex Kit (PN-120262) were used for all downstream RT, cDNA amplification (11 PCR cycles), and library preparation as instructed by the manufacturer (Chromium Next GEM Single Cell 3′ Reagent Kits v3.1 User Guide).

10x seq data processing and quality control

Libraries were sequenced on an Illumina HiSeq4000 or NovaSeq6000 (paired-end with read lengths of 150 bp) and Illumina sequencing reads were aligned to the mouse pre-mRNA reference transcriptome (mm10) using the 10x Genomics CellRanger pipeline (version 3.0.2) with default parameters. Cells that met any one of the following criteria were filtered out for downstream processing in each 10x run: less than 600 detected genes (for UMI count > 0), UMI counts exceeding 50,000 (potential multiplets), or proportion of the UMI count attributable to mitochondrial genes exceeding 15%. Doublets of different cell classes were further removed by first classifying cells into broad cell classes (neuronal versus nonneuronal) based on the co-expression of any pair of their marker genes (*Stmn2* for neurons; *Cldn5* for endothelial cells; *C1qc* for microglia; *Opalin* for oligodendrocytes; *Gja1* for astrocytes; *Pdgfra* for OPCs; *Mustn1* for mural cells). VMH cells are selected based on marker genes *Slc17a6*, *Adcyap1*, *Fezf1*, *Dlk1* and *Nr5a1*, as reported in our previous study [61].

Stereotaxic surgery

Surgeries were performed on adult *Npy2r^cre^*, *Esr1^cre^* or *Esr1^flp/+^Npy2r^cre/+^* mice aged 8–12 weeks. Mice were anaesthetized with isoflurane (0.8–5%) and placed on a stereotaxic frame (David Kopf Instruments). Virus was then injected into the target area using a pulled glass capillary (World Precision Instruments) and a pressure injector (Micro4 controller, World Precision

Instruments), at a flow rate of 20 nl/min. The injection volumes were 100-300 nl.

The Stereotaxic injection coordinates were based on the Paxinos and Franklin atlas (VMHvl, anterior–posterior: −4.68, medial–lateral: ±0.72, dorsal–ventral: −5.7). For optogenetic and fiber photometry experiments, single or dual optic fibers (optogenetics: diameter 200 μm, N.A., 0.22; fiber photometry: diameter 400 μm, N.A., 0.48; Doric lenses) were then placed above the virus injection sites (optogenetics: 500 μm above; fiber photometry: 150 μm above) and fixed on the skull with dental cement (Parkell). Mice were singly housed after surgery and were allowed to recover for at least 3 weeks before behavioral testing.

Fiber photometry

The fiber photometry setup was as previously described in earlier research [70] with minor modifications. We used 470 nm LEDs (M470F3, Thorlabs, filtered with 470-10 nm bandpass filters FB470-10, Thorlabs) for fluorophore excitation, and 405 nm LEDs for isosbestic excitation (M405FP1, Thorlabs, filtered with 410–10 nm bandpass filters FB410-10, Thorlabs). LEDs were modulated at 208 Hz (470 nm) and 333 Hz (405 nm) and controlled by a real-time processor (RZ5P, Tucker David Technologies) via an LED driver (DC4104, Thorlabs). The emission signal from the 470 nm excitation was normalized to the emission signal from the isosbestic excitation (405 nm), to control for motion artefacts, photobleaching and levels of GCaMP6m expression. LEDs were coupled to a 425 nm longpass dichroic mirror (Thorlabs, DMLP425R) via fiber optic patch cables (diameter 400 μm, N.A., 0.48; Doric lenses). Emitted light was collected via the patch cable, coupled to a 490 nm longpass dichroic mirror (DMLP490R, Thorlabs), filtered (FF01-542/27-25, Sem- rock), collimated through a focusing lens (F671SMA-405, Thorlabs) and detected by the photodetectors (Model 2151, Newport). Recordings were acquired using Synapse software (Tucker Davis Technologies).

On the test day, after at least 5 minutes of acclimation under the recording setup, the female was first recorded for 5 minutes to establish a baseline. Then behavior assays were proceeded and fluorescence were recorded for the indicated period of time, as described in the text.

All data analyses were performed in Python. Behavioral video files and fiber photometry data were time-locked. F_n was calculated using normalized (405 nm) fluorescence signals from 470 nm excitation. $F_n(t) = 100 \times [\ F_{470}(t) - F_{405fit}(t)\ ] / F_{405fit}(t)$. For the peri-event time histogram (PETH), the baseline value F_0 and standard deviation SD_0. was calculated using a -5 to -3 second window, except for the recordings of initial intruder encounters and first sniff of urine, where we used -30 to -20 second windows prior to each behavioral event. Overlapping behavioral bouts within this time window were excluded from the analysis. Then PETH was calculated by $[\ (F_n(t) - F_0)\ ] / SD_0$. The peak and areas under the PETH curve were calculated within the 3 second window, except for initial encounters and first sniff of urine, where we used a 30 second window and a 10 second window after onset of behavior, respectively. We confirmed that the latency to achieve PETH peak level is shorter than the indicated time window.

Optogenetics

Before initiating behavioral experiments, the light intensity achieved at the tip of the optic fiber was estimated by connecting an equivalent optic fiber to the patch cable and measuring the light intensity at the tip of the fiber using a power meter. Laser power was controlled by turning an analogue knob on the laser power supply. Mice were connected to a 445 nm laser or 593 nm laser (Changchun New Industries Optoelectronics Tech) via optical patch cords (diameter 200 µm, N.A., 0.22, Doric lenses and Thorlabs) and a rotary joint (Doric lenses). Mice were allowed to habituate to the cables after connecting them for at least 5 minutes before starting behavior tests. The experimenter monitored mouse behavior via a computer monitor in a room adjacent to the behavioral arena and triggered the laser manually.

For α cell silencing (Figure S4A-E) and activation (Figure 2A-G) in virgins, we repeatedly performed photostimulation bout consisting of a sham stimulation (OFF) trial and light stimulation (ON) trial, for 30 minutes or up to male ejaculation. Bouts were separated by a ~30 second interval. The whole bout would be excluded if no male mounting attempt occurred during any of the two trials. For α cell activation (Figure 2H-K) and β cell silencing (Figure 3A-E) in lactating females and β cell activation in virgin (Figure 3F-P) and lactating females (Figure S4F-J), we alternately delivered sham stimulation (OFF) trials and light stimulation (ON) trials when animals were engaged in the behaviors of interest, during equivalent behavioral epochs, with at least a two-minute interval between trials. The detailed frequency and duration of photostimulation for each trial were indicated in the Figures and were controlled using an Accupulse Generator (World Precision Instruments) or an Isolated Pulse Stimulator (A-M Systems).

To determine the estrus phases of tested females, vaginal smear cytology was applied on the same day as the behavior test. A vaginal smear was collected immediately after the behavioral test and stained with 0.1% crystal violet solution for 1 minute. Cell types in the stained vaginal smear were checked microscopically. In this study, the estrus phase was characterized by many cornified epithelial cells and no leukocytes. Diestrus was characterized by many leukocytes.

Histology

Once the behavioral experiments were finished, virus expression and implant placement were histologically verified on all mice. Mice lacking correct virus expression or implant placement were excluded from the analysis. Mice were transcardially perfused with 1x PBS at room temperature, followed by 4% paraformaldehyde (PFA) (diluted from 16% EM grade PFA). Brains were extracted and post-fixed in 4% PFA 16-24h at 4°C, followed by 24 hours in 30% sucrose/PBS at 4 °C. Brains were embedded in OCT mounting medium, frozen on dry ice and stored at −80°C for subsequent sectioning. Brains were sectioned into 60-100 μm slices on a cryostat (Leica Biosystems). Sections were washed with 1× PBS and mounted on Superfrost slides, then incubated for 15 minutes at room temperature in DAPI/PBS (0.5 µg/ml) for counterstaining, washed again and coverslipped. Sections were imaged with an epifluorescent microscope (Olympus VS120)

QUANTIFICATION AND STATISTICAL ANALYSIS

All data were analyzed blind to relevant variables including estrous cycle, treatment, genotype (mice and virus), and light illumination conditions. Statistical analysis was performed using GraphPad PRISM (GraphPad Software). We first determined sample distribution normality using Kolmogorov–Smirnov tests. In experiments with paired samples, we used a paired t test and a Wilcoxon rank test for parametric and non-parametric data, respectively. In all other experiments, we used an unpaired t test and Mann-Whitney U-test for parametric and non-parametric data, respectively. Supplemental Table 1 states our sample sizes and definitions as well as precision measures.

10x Data analysis and clustering

All downstream analysis of Act-seq 10x scRNA-seq data was performed with R package Seurat (v3.1.3) [80]. The 10x gene expression matrices from all samples were combined as one Seurat object for analysis. We filtered cells with feature counts over 50000, UMIs less than 600, or mitochondrial UMIs exceeding 15%. For each remaining cell, gene expression was normalized by total number of counts, multiplied by a scale factor (10,000), and logtransformed (NormalizeData function). Then, 2000 highly variable genes were identified (FindVariableGenes function; top 2,000 genes with the highest standardized variance selected by selection.method = 'vst') after removing immediate early genes (e.g., *Fos, Fosl2, Junb*; 139 genes in total from [63]). The gene expression levels of those 2000 genes were scaled relative to the proportion of mitochondrial UMIs and total molecular counts of each cell (regressed out) (ScaleData function). Next, we applied principal component analysis (PCA) to reduce dimensionality; the first 40 PCs were used to generate clusters (FindNeighbors function; FindClusters function). Specifically, we performed iterative rounds of clustering and cell selection. For the first round, we distinguished neuronal cells from non-neuronal cells using marker genes (*Stmn2* for neurons; *Cldn5* for endothelial cells; *C1qc* for microglia; *Opalin* for oligodendrocytes; *Gja1* for astrocytes; *Pdgfra* for OPCs; *Mustn1* for mural cells). For the second round, we selected VMH cells using marker genes *Slc17a6*, *Adcyap1*, *Fezf1*, *Dlk1* and *Nr5a1* (reported in Kim et al., 2019). 19,103 VMH cells were clustered into 27 transcriptomic cell types (resolution 1.5). Clustering robustness for VMH clusters was evaluated by varying the resolution (1–2). Cluster identification was robust across the range of resolutions.

VMH transcriptomic data integration

To map female ventral VMH transcriptomic cell types onto the male dataset (Kim et al.,

2019), we performed data integration using Seurat v3.1.3 [80]. Briefly,
we selected the top 2,000 genes with the highest dispersion (variance to mean ratio) from each dataset (male-VMH-SMART-seq: 3,850 neurons; male-VMH-10x: 41,182 neurons; female-VMH-10x: 19,103 neurons) and took the union of these resulting gene sets. After removing unwanted genes (sex-specific, immediate early, retro-virus-induced, and noisesensitive genes; as described in Kim et al., 2019), 3,049 genes were used as input to identify the pairwise correspondences between single cells across two different datasets, called anchors (FindIntegrationAnchors function; normalization.method = "LogNormalize"; first 75 PCs were used; male-VMH-10x was used as reference data during integration). We then used these anchors to integrate the datasets together (IntegrateData function; normalization.method = "LogNormalize"; first 75 PCs were used) and performed a joint clustering on these aligned embeddings (FindNeighbors function with first 75 PCs followed by FindClusters function with resolution 1.5), yielding 38 clusters (referred to as "Integrated cell types"; Figures S3A,B).

Chapter 3

THE DYNAMICS OF FEMALE MATING RECEPTIVITY ARE ENCODED BY A HYPOTHALAMIC LINE ATTRACTOR

Liu, M.+, Nair, A.+, Linderman, S.W., & Anderson, D. J. (2023). Periodic hypothalamic attractor-like dynamics during the estrus cycle. *biorxiv, (in revision),* https://doi.org/10.1101/2023.05.22.541741

Summary

Females display complex and dynamic behaviors during mating interactions and exhibit variable sexual receptivity in different hormonal states. However, how the dynamics of mating behavior and receptivity are encoded in the female brain remains largely unknown. The ventromedial hypothalamus, ventro-lateral subdivision (VMHvl) contains a transcriptomically distinct subpopulation of estrogen receptor type 1 (Esr1)-positive neurons that causally control mating receptivity in female mice. Unsupervised linear dynamical systems analysis of single-cell calcium imaging data from these neurons in receptive female mice during mating uncovered a dimension with slow ramping activity, generating an approximate line attractor in neural state space. During a mating interaction, the neural population vector progressed gradually along this attractor, escalating to a peak just before male ejaculation and then dropped rapidly. Within-subject longitudinal imaging across the estrus cycle revealed that attractor dynamics can appear and disappear in a receptive state and hormone-dependent manner. Furthermore, the level of activity in the integration dimension was strongly and positively correlated with variation in the level of female receptivity both within and across animals. These observations suggest that a hypothalamic line attractor may encode a persistent and escalating state of female sexual arousal or engagement during mating, and that it can be reversibly modulated by hormonal states on a timescale of days.

Introduction

Mating is a complex social interaction whose success is essential to species' survival. In rodents, female mating receptivity has been considered as a simple binary switch that is defined by the expression of lordosis[81–84], a reflexive acceptance posture, during interactions with a male. In fact, however, female receptivity is highly dynamic: it exhibits variability both within a mating interaction and across different physiological states[85]. Nevertheless, the female's important contribution to the dynamics of successful mating has been underappreciated and under-studied, while these dynamics have been analyzed primarily from a male-centric viewpoint.

Recent progress has identified circuit-level mechanisms that control female receptivity[16,17,86,87]. The ventrolateral subdivision of the ventromedial hypothalamic nucleus (VMHvl) contains a subset of Esr1$^+$ neurons that controls mating behaviors in female mice[5– 7,29,39,40]. Recent findings have revealed receptivity-dependent changes in the anatomy and physiology of these neurons. The axonal arborizations of VMHvl progesterone receptor (PR)-expressing neurons in in AVPV increase in receptive females, in an estrogen-dependent manner[53]. More recently, a small subset of Esr1$^+$ neurons defined by expression of the CCK receptor (*Cckar*)[7,57] has been shown to be necessary and sufficient for female receptivity, and to exhibit estrus cycle-dependent changes in its excitability[7]. While these studies have uncovered important changes associated with female receptivity *per se*, how the dynamics of female receptivity and mating behavior are encoded in the brain is largely unknown.

To address this issue systematically, we sought to characterize neural representations in female VMHvl during mating interactions and across the estrus cycle, using miniscope imaging of neuronal calcium activity[88] in freely behaving animals. We imaged a subpopulation of Esr1$^+$ neurons that are Npy2r$^-$ that we call "α cells," whose activity is functionally essential for and able to promote sexual receptivity[6]; these cells overlap with the Cckar$^+$ cells independently identified in other studies[6,7]. We performed longitudinal singlecell imaging of VMHvl α cells in naturally cycling or ovariectomized hormonesupplemented females during multiple unrestrained interactions with sexually experienced males. Unsupervised modeling of VMHvl α cell activity using a linear dynamical systems approach[89] revealed an approximate line attractor in neural state space, which disappears during non-receptive phases of the estrus cycle and is hormone-dependent. Quantitative analysis of female mating behavior and line attractor dynamics suggest that the attractor may represent or encode a persistent, escalating internal state of female sexual arousal or receptivity during mating.

Results

The dynamics of female behaviors during mating interactions

Female mating behavior has been studied extensively in rats but less so in mice[87,90]. To characterize murine female mating behavior under our standard conditions in detail, we manually annotated multiple video recordings (5-10 min each) of sexually receptive females interacting with a male (Fig. 1a). We identified a set of 10 female motor behaviors and classified them semantically as appetitive (comprising approaching and sniffing the male), accepting (comprising lordosis and wiggling), or resisting (comprising darting, top up, kicking and turning), according to the apparent intent of the behavior[7]. The expression of these behaviors was dynamic, with the probability of accepting behaviors displaying a gradual increase, while resistance behaviors initially increased and then slowly decreased (Fig. 1b and Extended Data Fig. 1a). Thus, receptivity is not binary but graded and dynamic.

We also categorized these mating behaviors as either "self-initiated" (comprising appetitive and check genital area) or "male-responsive" (behaviors responsive to male mating attempts, comprising accepting, resistance and staying). We found that females spent six times longer displaying male-responsive (83.9%) vs. self-initiated behaviors (16.1%) (Fig. 1c). Because of this strong asymmetry, we also quantified male-initiated mating behaviors (comprising sniffing, mounting and intromission). During each interaction, the male spent 11.3 times more time than the female displaying self-initiated mating behaviors (Fig. 1d). Thus, males largely drive the progression of a mating interaction. Notably, the number and duration of male copulation bouts and inter-bouts intervals varied across interactions (Fig. 1e and Extended Data Fig. 1b).

Next, we compared female behaviors during male copulation bouts vs. inter-bout intervals
(Fig. 1f). To simplify reporting of this analysis, we classified behaviors as either "social" (comprising accepting, resisting, and appetitive), or as "disengaged" (non-social; comprising rearing, digging, and chewing). During copulation bouts, females primarily exhibited social behaviors (62% of each bout's duration) and rarely showed disengaged behaviors (Fig. 1g, left). Notably, during inter-copulation bout intervals (IBIs), when females were physically separated from the males, they exhibited persistent social behaviors initiated during the preceding copulation bout (Fig. 1g, right, 23% of IBI duration). A plot of behavior probability aligned to copulation offset revealed that females continued displaying accepting or resisting behaviors, and performed appetitive approaches and sniffing of interacting males during IBIs (Fig. 1h and Extended Data Fig. 1c).

Taken together, these results demonstrate that female behaviors during mating are dynamic and primarily driven by responses to male-initiated behaviors. Importantly, the persistence of female social behaviors observed during sporadic male-initiated pauses in copulation (Fig. 1h) is suggestive of a corresponding persistent internal state of mating receptivity or engagement. The ramping dynamics of "accepting" behaviors (Fig. 1b) further suggests that escalation may be a property of this internal state as well. Persistence and escalation (or "scalability") are features of internal states underlying other dynamic social behaviors such as male aggression[91]. In what follows we investigate the instantiation of these state properties by neural activity and dynamics.

Tuning properties of female VMHvl neurons during mating

To uncover how the dynamics of female mating behavior are encoded in neural activity, we imaged VMHvl[Esr1+,Npy2r-] ("α") cells[6] in freely moving sexually receptive females interacting with males, using a miniature head-mounted microscope[88] (Fig. 2a). Initially, we analyzed responses observed in the first minute of exposure to either a male or female conspecific (Extended Data Fig. 2a). We observed distinct subsets of α cells tuned to male or female conspecifics, with male-preferring cells ~4 times more abundant (Extended Data Fig. 2b). Correspondingly, the averaged population response to a male was ~4 times higher than that to a female (Extended Data Fig. 2c), consistent with prior bulk calcium imaging studies[6]. Principal component analysis (PCA) of these data revealed a clear separation of intruder sex in the first two dimensions (Extended Data Fig. 2d).

We next analyzed imaging data from females acquired during free mating interactions with a male, over 5-10 min observation periods (Fig. 2b; 16-207 units/mouse, mean 89±12= units/mouse; N = 15 mice). First, we performed choice probability analysis[74] to compare the relative tuning of neurons with respect to pairs of selected behaviors. This indicated that a relatively small percentage of VMHvl α cells (~2-13%) were "tuned" to specific mating behaviors (Fig. 2c and Extended Data Fig. 3a, b), while the majority exhibited "mixed selectivity" (Fig. 2c and Extended Data Fig. 3a, b, gray bars), indicating relatively weak behavior-specific tuning at the single neuron level.

To further investigate the relationship between mating behaviors and neural activity, we fit Generalized Linear Models (GLMs) to the activity of each neuron as a weighted sum of either female mating behaviors (Fig. 2d), male mating behaviors (Extended Data Fig. 3c), or both female and male behaviors (Extended Data Fig. 3d). We observed both neurons poorly fit ($cvR^2 \ll ~0.5$) and well-fit (cross validated R^2 (cvR^2) $\geq$ ~0.5) by GLMs (Extended Data Fig. 3e). Across all animals, only ~8% of the variance in neural activity was explained by female mating behaviors (Fig. 2e, mean cvR^2=0.08, N=15 mice); ~14% of the variance was explained by male mating behaviors (Extended Data Fig. 3c, mean cvR^2=0.14) and ~15% of the variance was explained by combined female and male behaviors (Extended Data Fig. 3d, mean cvR^2=0.15).

Taken together, these single-cell analyses indicated that a large fraction of the variance in VMHvl α-cell neural activity during female mating could not be explained by behavior using a GLM. Nevertheless, a trained SVM linear decoder could distinguish mating behaviors with an accuracy higher than chance (Extended Data Fig. 4), suggesting some relationship between neural activity or dynamics and behavior. To examine whether local interactions between neurons could improve the fit of our GLMs, we included coupling filters[92,93] in addition to the behavioral variables (Fig. 2f). The introduction of neuronal coupling dramatically increased variance explained by the GLM, suggesting that local circuit interactions contribute more than behavior to neuronal variance in VMHvl α cell activity (Fig. 2f, g, mean cvR^2=0.46, N = 15 mice). Because GLMs fit using low-dimensional coupling matrices (as obtained here) can reflect slowly evolving neural dynamics, we were motivated to analyze next the dynamics of VMHvl α cell activity.

Neural dynamics in female VMHvl during mating
We first examined the dynamics of single neuron activity by measuring the half-width of each neuron's autocorrelation function[74] (ACHW), an approximation of the neuron's time constant[94,95] (Fig. 3a). This analysis identified individual cells that exhibited apparent persistent activity across the mating interaction. Thirty percent of cells displayed ACHWs longer than 25 seconds (mean ACHW: 20s, Fig. 3b), a duration longer than the mean copulation IBI (13.7s, Fig. 1e, *right*). Notably, the ACHW of the same female cells was significantly lower when the male was confined in a perforated enclosure (pencil cup), than during free mating interaction (mean ACHW for pencil cup: 14.3 ± 0.42s, mean ACHW for free interaction: 19.64 ± 0.58s,

Extended Data Fig. 6a-c), suggesting that the latter cannot be fully explained by persistent male odors (which should be detectable by the female even when the male is enclosed in the pencil cup).

Given that the single cell analysis revealed evidence of persistent neural activity, we considered whether a systems-level approach could capture low-dimensional features of population neural dynamics. To this end we fit an unsupervised (i.e., without reference to any behavioral annotation) linear dynamical systems model (recurrent Switching Linear Dynamical Systems, rSLDS[89,91]) directly to neural data during individual trials (Fig. 3c, f, g; N=15 mice, mean variance explained (calculated as cvR^2 between observed and predicted neural trajectories: 64.08 ± 6.8%). Recurrent SLDS approximates a non-linear system as a combination of several discrete linear dynamical systems, or "states". The model simplified neural activity by dimensionally reducing it to a few continuous latent factors, similar to
PCA. This approach captures the tendency of population activity to lie near a low dimensional linear manifold in neural state-space and describes how it evolves over time. The structure of the manifold is "learned" by a machine learning algorithm that fits a linear dynamics matrix for each state. The eigenvalues of this fit dynamics matrix yield the time constants of population activity for each of the latent factors (dimensions) in a given state.

Applying rSLDS analysis to VMHvl α-cell activity revealed that one of the dimensions in state S2 exhibited a relatively long time constant (which reflects the rate at which activity decays in response to a transient increase along this dimension), in comparison to the other dimensions (110.7±13.6s; Fig. 3d, red dot, 3e, N = 15 mice). Examining the $\log_2$ ratio of the two longest time constants to calculate a so-called "line attractor score"[91] revealed that the fit dynamical system contains a line attractor (see Fig. 3g, below), which is aligned in neural state-space to the dimension with the longest time constant. For convenience we refer hereafter to this dimension as the "integration" dimension[15]. Across multiple mice (N=15), the average variance in neural activity explained by these rSLDS models was higher than that explained by our GLMs (64 ± 7%, 74% for example mouse shown; see Extended Data Fig. 5i-l for further examples).

To investigate the existence of an integration dimension in the system independently of the fit rSLDS model, we used a complementary method, supervised targeted dimensionality reduction (partial least squares regression)[74]. This approach, which used ramping activity as a regressor, was able to identify a dimension whose slow dynamics were very well correlated with those of the rSLDS integration dimension (r^2~0.92-0.94; Extended Data Fig. 5m, n). This result confirmed that slow integration dynamics is indeed a property of a subset of
VMHvl neurons, one that is not dependent on the particulars of the rSLDS fitting algorithm.

We next visualized the dynamics of the activity of cells contributing to the integration dimension as a weighted average over time, in order to compare it to annotated mating behaviors. This analysis revealed ramping activity that began to increase at the onset of sniffing, mounting, or intromission (depending on the trial), and which continued to increase across multiple mating bouts and IBIs (Fig. 3f and Extended Data Fig. 5). Analysis of the traces of individual neurons contributing to (weighted by) the integration dimension indicated that some single cells exhibited ramping-like activity (Extended Data Fig. 6d, e, 56% of neurons r^2 >0.5), but that different cells peaked at different times during the mating interaction (Extended Data Fig. 6f, g, orange arrowheads). This suggests that the robust ramping activity seen in the integration dimension (Extended Data Fig. 6f, upper) is an emergent property of the population and not solely a collective property of all single neurons.

To visualize the flow field of the rSLDS-fit dynamical system we projected it into a 2dimensional state space using PCA (Fig. 3g). This projection revealed a stable region (white area) comprising a linear array of "slow points" that approximated a line attractor (Fig. 3g-i). The orientation of this array largely reflected its value with respect to the second principal component (Fig. 3g, PC_2), which is primarily contributed by the slow (ramping) dimension of the rSLDS model (Fig. 3f). Mapping annotated behaviors onto the neural trajectory in this state space indicated that the population vector entered the line attractor following initial close contact with the male and progressed along it during successive male intromission bouts (Fig. 3h, i). This progression reflects the ramping seen in the integration dimension discovered by rSLDS (Fig. 3f and Extended Data Fig. 5). Notably, in some animals the neural vector exhibited brief, loop-like excursions orthogonal to the attractor dimension during IBIs (Fig. 3i; Extended Data Fig. 5d, h, l), suggesting "attractiveness" of the observed fixed points against either natural perturbations orthogonal to the attractor, or noise.

The presence of a putative line attractor suggested a mechanism to stably maintain population activity in a particular state during interruptions or pauses in male mating behavior. To test this hypothesis, we first examined activity during copulation inter-bout intervals, when the male is physically separated from the female. Notably, we found that the average value of the integration dimension during copulation IBIs was relatively high, similar to and statistically indistinguishable from that measured during the preceding copulation bout (Fig. 3j). Accordingly it was not possible, using activity in this dimension, to train a decoder to distinguish videoframes containing copulation bouts vs. IBIs with accuracy greater than chance (Fig. 3k).

To further probe the stability of the identified line attractor in female VMHvl, we next carried out behavioral perturbation experiments to non-invasively and transiently interrupt male mating (Fig. 3l). After several successful intromission bouts had been performed, we remotely abrogated copulation by optogenetic activation of VMHdm^{Sf1+} cells in males, which promoted an abrupt defensive state[96,97]. During the laser-on period, males stopped all mating behaviors, including singing, and displayed no active approach to the female. The induced mating pauses lasted for several minutes (1-5 mins), which were much longer than the natural mating pauses (Fig. 1f; average IBI = 13.7s). Nevertheless, activity in the integration dimension in the female brain remained elevated for minutes while the male was prevented from resuming mating (Fig. 3m), consistent with the persistent activity we observed during the natural male copulation pauses (Fig. 3j).

Together, these data indicated that VMHvl α cell activity displays approximate line attractor dynamics during mating, and that the stability of the system in the integration dimension does not require continuous male contact-dependent sensory input. In further support of this conclusion, in a cohort of naturally cycling females exhibiting variable receptivity (see below), we obtained some trials with high male intromission rates but low female receptivity behavior (Fig. 3p, colored dots, Videos). Notably, analysis of those trials revealed relatively little if any ramping in the integration dimension (Fig. 3q). These data suggest that ramping does not simply reflect accumulated mechanosensory inputs derived from male intromission.

Lastly, we sought to identify a correlate of the ramping activity revealed by line attractor dynamics in VMHvl (Fig. 3f). Males display sequential mating behaviors with escalating intensity from sniffing to mounting, intromission and finally ejaculation, reflecting an escalating internal state of sexual arousal. One might imagine, therefore that a corresponding increase in the level of female sexual arousal might occur in parallel, in order to encourage successful sperm transfer and fertilization. If such arousal were encoded by the ramping activity, then one would predict that this activity should abruptly terminate or decrease following male climax. Indeed, activity in the integration dimension peaked just prior to ejaculation, and immediately dropped thereafter (Fig. 3n, o).

Line attractor dynamics encode female sexual receptivity across days.

If the line attractor observed during mating indeed reflects or encodes the level of female receptivity, one would predict that it should be altered in some way, or even absent, when females are in an unreceptive state. We tested this hypothesis in two ways. First, we performed longitudinal imaging in multiple females (N = 4 mice) across their 4-5 day estrus cycle, during which receptivity changes (Extended Data Fig. 7a). In each animal, we were able to obtain data from 1 sexually receptive day and 2 unreceptive days and to align neurons from those recordings across days (Fig. 4a). Consistent with previous studies[6,53], no change in average VMHvl α cell population activity (triggered on male mounting attempt) was apparent on receptive vs. unreceptive days (Extended Data Fig. 7b). However, raster plots revealed obvious differences in the pattern of single-unit activity on receptive vs. unreceptive days (Fig. 4a, *right*).

To determine whether there were also differences in VMHvl α cell dynamics across the estrus cycle, we fit rSLDS models to data obtained on both receptive and unreceptive days, for each individual. Models fit to data from unreceptive days failed to identify a single dimension with a very long time constant, indicating the absence of a line attractor (Fig. 4b, c). Accordingly, the first 2 PCs of rSLDS state-space did not exhibit integration-like activity, but rather relatively fast dynamics time-locked to male sniffing and mounting (PC2 in Fig. 4d). In 2D flow-field projections, neural state space contained a single point attractor, reflecting stable baseline activity prior to interaction with the male, from which the population vector made rapid excursions during sniffing and mounting (Fig. 4e, f).

To compare neural dynamics on non-receptive vs. receptive days more directly, we projected neural activity from unreceptive days into the rSLDS model fit to data from the receptive day using the same neurons aligned across days (Fig. 4g). The projected neural data failed to show ramping behavior in the 1st rSLDS dimension (Fig. 4h). Accordingly, in 2D projections of the flow-field the neural population activity vector remained outside of the line attractor (Extended Data

Fig. 8b, c). Importantly, although male mounting occurred on unreceptive days (Fig. 4h, purple rasters), activity in the 1st rSLDS dimension was low during this behavior (Extended Data Fig. 8d), indicating that it is not sufficient to explain the ramping observed on receptive days.

These results suggested that a change in neural dynamics occurred between receptive and unreceptive days. This inference was supported by the lower autocorrelation half-width (ACHW) of cells weighted on the 1st rSLDS dimension on unreceptive vs. receptive days (Extended Data Fig. 9a, b; distribution mean for ACHW on unreceptive days 16.1 ± 0.8s; on receptive days 25.2 ± 1.5s, p<0.001). This difference in mean ACHW was observed regardless of the order in which receptive and unreceptive days occurred in different mice (Extended Data Fig. 9c, f, i). Neurons that did not contribute to the 1st rSLDS dimension did not exhibit a change in ACHW (Extended Data Fig. 9d, g). Finally, we compared the ACHWs of each individual unit on receptive vs. non-receptive days. A scatterplot of these data revealed a subpopulation (39 ± 5%) of line attractor-weighted neurons whose ACHW was higher on receptive than on unreceptive days (Extended Data Fig. 9e, h, red datapoints).

As a second independent test of the hypothesis that the line attractor encodes receptivity, we subjected a cohort of females to ovariectomy (OVX) to render them unreceptive, and performed longitudinal imaging in the OVX animals before vs. after hormone priming to restore receptivity (daily injection of estrogen (E) + progesterone (P) in oil; OVX/EP; controls injected with oil only). The results indicated that attractor dynamics disappeared following OVX and were reinstated following hormone-priming (Extended Data Fig. 10j). The females used in this cohort had also been imaged during their natural cycle, and fit with rSLDS models. In some individuals, the model fit on receptive days was not as good as in other animals (Extended Data Fig. 10k, "forward simulation accuracy"). Strikingly, in one such animal the fit of the rSLDS model was strikingly improved following OVX and hormone priming, compared to the fit obtained on her naturally receptive day (Extended Data Fig. 10k vs. l). Taken together, these data confirm a strong prediction of the hypothesis that the line attractor observed during mating encodes some aspect of mating receptivity.

The foregoing data left open the important question of whether the continuous lowdimensional variable instantiated by the line attractor reflects or encodes continuous variation in the degree of female receptivity. In males, differences in the time constant of the integration dimension are strongly correlated with differences in aggressiveness, across individual animals[19]. We therefore sought to examine line attractor parameters within a cohort of females exhibiting individual differences in receptivity across trials and days. To generate this cohort, we injected naturally cycling females with estrogen (but not progesterone) daily beginning 2 days before imaging, and continued the injections during 37 days of repeated imaging of the same animals during daily mating tests (N = 6 mice). These injections increased the number of days on which females exhibited receptivity, while still allowing variation in the level of receptivity (as measured by the amount of accepting behaviors displayed in a given trial) in response to changing levels of endogenous sex hormones across the estrus cycle (Fig. 4i, j and Extended Data Fig. 11a). This design afforded the opportunity to correlate quantitative variation in receptivity with variation in line attractor parameters.

We fit rSLDS models to imaging data from each animal and mating trial and plotted the average activity of the integration dimension over time (cf. Fig. 4h, receptive day 3). Strikingly, the area under this curve (auc) was strongly and positively correlated with the percentage of time that females performed accepting behaviors during each mating interaction (Fig. 4k, l; r^2=0.62). In contrast, other behaviors such as resistance and appetitive behaviors were not correlated with this measure (Extended Data Fig. 11b). These data indicate that variation in movement along the line attractor reflects variation in levels of sexual receptivity, across individuals and trials.

Discussion

Mating is a complex and dynamic social interaction. How the brain encodes the dynamics of female sexual behavior within or across mating interactions is largely unknown. Using unsupervised dynamical system modeling of neural data, we have discovered an approximate line attractor that emerges from population activity in a genetically defined subset of VMHvl^{Esr1} neurons that causally control female mating receptivity. We suggest that this attractor represents or encodes a persistent, scalable internal state of female sexual arousal or receptivity. These neural dynamics vary periodically during the estrus cycle, and scale with individual differences in receptivity. To our knowledge, there is no prior example of a line attractor that appears and disappears with periodic changes in behavioral/hormonal state on a time scale of days.

Line attractor dynamics can afford internal states two important features: stability (persistence) and ramping (scalability). These two properties may enable important aspects of female receptivity behavior dynamics. Stability may allow females to cope with the sporadic, intermittent and protracted nature of male copulation, which can last for tens of minutes or more. The rapidity with which males successfully re-initated copulation following natural or experimentally induced interruptions suggests that the female has a mechanism to maintain her sexual arousal during unpredictable pauses in male mating, until ejaculation is achieved. The stability of the line attractor may function to maintain the female in a persistently aroused state during intermittent male copulatory bouts. This interpretation is supported by evidence of persistent neural activity in the integration dimension spanning bouts of copulation and their IBIs (Fig. 3j, k). It is also supported by our observation that female social behavior continues for some time following natural interruptions in copulation (Extended Data Fig. 1c)

Ramping may afford the female adaptation to the escalation of male sexual arousal required to achieve ejaculation. In principle, anything that the female can do to facilitate that escalation should increase the probability that the male will successfully transfer his sperm and fertilize her eggs. The ramping activity exhibited in the integration dimension is suggestive of a continuous, escalating variable in the female brain that reflects or is coordinated with the dynamics of male sexual arousal. The simplest interpretation is that this variable encodes the level of female sexual arousal. Consistent with this interpretation, ramping peaked just prior to ejaculation and immediately dropped thereafter (Fig. 3n, o). Thus, these two characteristic features of a line attractor – its stability and its ability to encode a low-dimensional continuous variable – provide an attractive neural instantiation of two key features inherent in the dynamics of female mating receptivity.

The idea that the line attractor encodes mating receptivity is supported by its presence or absence during receptive vs. unreceptive estrus cycle days or in ovariectomized females with vs. without hormone priming, respectively (Fig. 4c). Importantly, however, it is not just a binary correlate of receptivity: the degree of movement along the attractor was highly correlated ($r^2=0.62$) with the level of receptivity as measured by the frequency of accepting behaviors (Fig. 4k and Extended Data Fig. 11b). In contrast, the integration dimension was not well-correlated with other female behaviors. Whether neural dynamics distinguishing these behaviors exist in other dimensions is an interesting topic for future study.

An important question is whether ramping is intrinsic to the network or input-driven, for example by repetitive mounting or intromission. Several instances were observed wherein males performed intromission despite the absence of female receptive behavior (suggestive of a "non-consensual" mating interaction; Fig. 3p). Importantly, in such cases intromission was not accompanied by ramping activity in the integration dimension (Fig. 3q). These data argue that ramping activity cannot be driven exclusively by mechanosensory input from intromission bouts. However, we cannot exclude that such input contributes to ramping when females are receptive.

Mating is sexually dimorphic, both behaviorally and in its underlying neural circuitry[98]. MPOA causally controls mating behaviors in males[4], while VMHvl controls it in females[67]. In contrast to the line attractor identified in female VMHvl, dynamical systems modeling of male MPOA[Esr1] neuronal activity during mating[4,74] revealed a rotational trajectory, in which different steps in mating behavior occurred at different characteristic angles of rotation[91].

The finding that males and females use different neural dynamics to encode their mating behaviors may be adaptive for successful fertilization. Male behavior drives mating interactions and has to progress from mounting to intromission to ejaculation (Fig. 1d). The rotational dynamics observed in MPOA may facilitate stepwise and sequential mating action selection in males. In contrast, during the lengthy period required to achieve ejaculation, females must maintain an aroused state in the face of sporadic and unpredictable interruptions in male copulatory behavior. Line attractor dynamics may be well-adapted to facilitate the maintenance of this internal motive or sexual arousal state. We note, however, that line attractor dynamics are also observed in male VMHvl during mating[91] and may encode maintenance or escalation of male sexual arousal as well.

The nature of the different α cell subpopulations that underlie receptive state-dependent attractor dynamics remains to be determined. Our previous work has shown that transcriptionally distinct subsets of VMHvl[Esr1] neurons, called α and β cells, control female sexual receptivity and maternal aggression, respectively[6]. Here we show that the α cell population exhibits further heterogeneity at the physiological level, comprising subpopulations that do or do not contribute to the line attractor. Whether these subpopulations are transcriptomically distinct is not yet clear[7,57] and will require further study. Recently, it was reported that a subset of the α cell population expressing Cckar

(VMHvl^{Cckar} neurons) displayed receptivity-associated changes in spontaneous activity and responsivity to male cues *in vivo*, as well as in their excitability and synaptic input *in vitro*[7]. Whether these cells and their state-dependent physiological changes contribute to the reversible line attractor dynamics observed here requires further investigation.

Taken together, our results suggest that neural population dynamics encode the dynamics of female mating receptivity and can be reversibly sculpted by physiological state. They also provide further evidence in support of the general concept that line attractors encode internal states underlying innate social behaviors[21]. Because the cellular, molecular and connectional features of VMHvl are well-described[5,6,27,29,61,75], this system may provide an opportunity to understand how hormones, genes, cell types and local circuitry generate emergent neural population dynamics that underlie innate social behaviors.

Figures

Fig. 1 Dynamics of female behaviors during mating interaction.

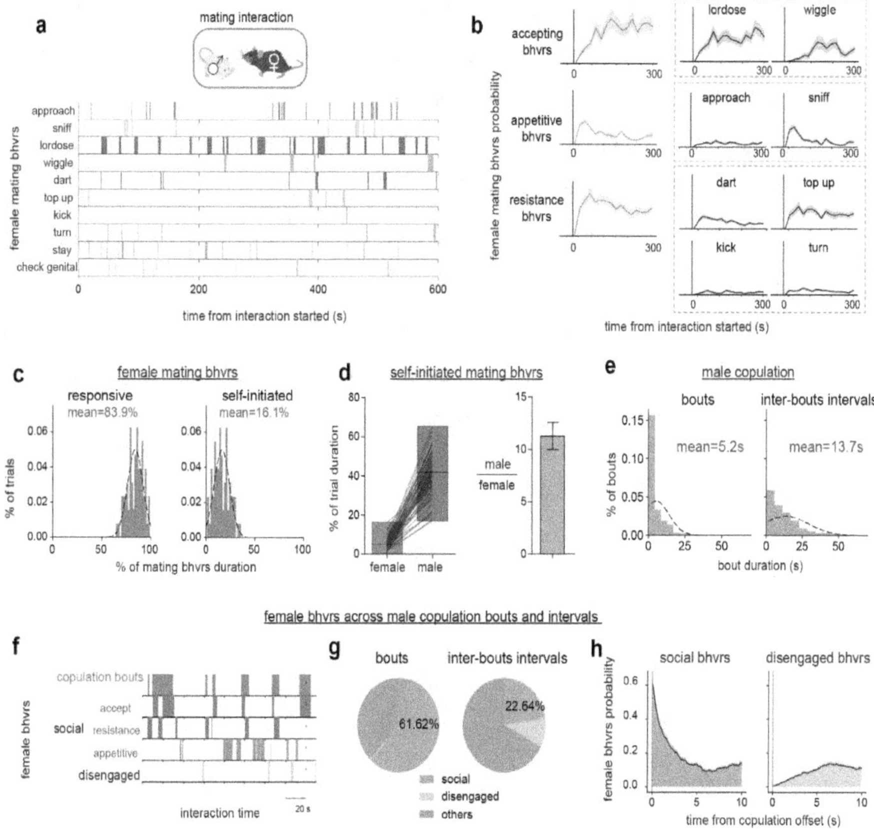

Figure 1. | Dynamics of female behaviors during mating interaction.

a, Raster plot of 10 female mating behaviors during one interaction with a male. **b**, The probability of mating behaviors during every 20 seconds (n=74 trials, N=28 mice). Behaviors were grouped as accept (comprising lordose, wiggle), appetitive (comprising approach, sniff), and resistance (comprising dart, top up, kick and turn). **c,** Distribution of the percentage of time females displayed responsive vs. self-initiated mating behaviors over the total mating behavior time in each trial (n=74 trials). Female self-initiated mating behaviors comprised appetitive behaviors and check genital. Female responsive mating behaviors comprised accepting, resistance behaviors and staying. **d**, Left, percentage of time female or male displayed self-initiated mating behaviors in each trial. Right, male self-initiated mating time over female in each trial (n=74 trials). Male selfinitiated mating behaviors included male sniffing, mounting and intromission. **e,** Distribution of the durations of male copulation bouts (left, n=1685) and inter-bout intervals (right) (n=1611). Male copulation included mounting and intromission. **f,** Raster plot of female behaviors during copulation bouts and inter-bout intervals. Social behaviors comprised accepting, resistance, and appetitive behaviors; non-social disengaged behaviors comprised rearing, digging and chewing. **g,** Percentage of time female displaying social behaviors in each male copulation bout or inter-bout interval; "others" indicates all behaviors other than the defined social behaviors or non-social disengaged behaviors during interaction. **h,** Female behavior probability aligned to male copulation offsets.

Fig. 2 Tuning properies of female VHMvl neurons during mating.

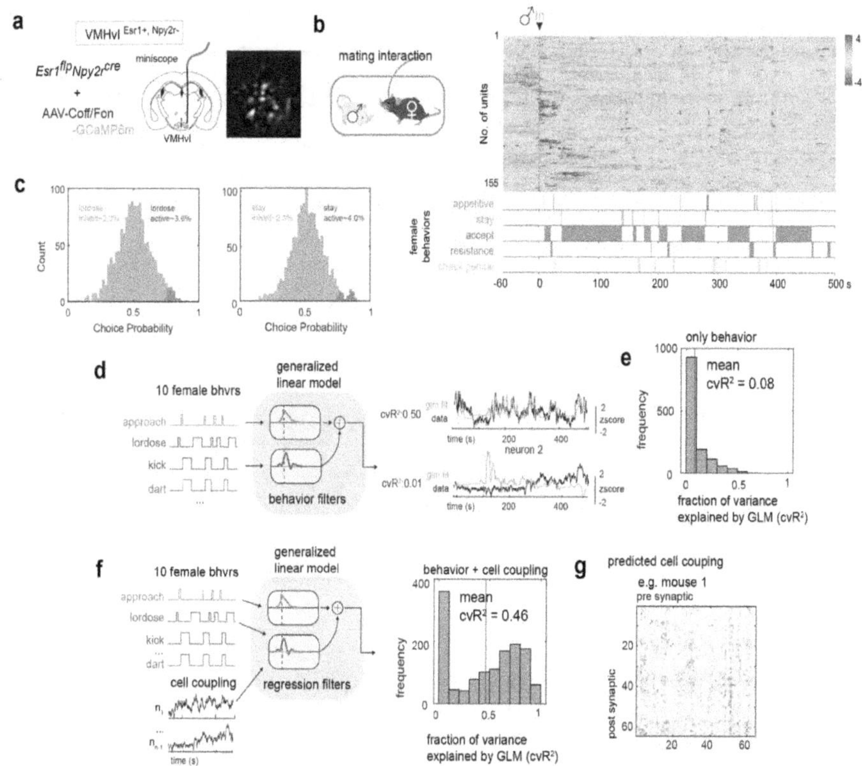

Figure 2 | Tuning properties of female VMHvl neurons during mating.

a, Left, schematic illustrating miniscope imaging of female VMHvl[Esr1+,Npy2r-] (α) cells; Right, an example imaging plane. **b**, Diagram illustrating mating interaction test. Single cell responses during mating interaction (top) and their corresponding behaviors (bottom), from one example female. Units were sorted by temporal correlation. Color scale indicates z-scored activity. **c**, Choice Probability (CP) histograms and percentages of tuned cells. cutoff: CP>0.7 or <0.3 and >2σ. (N = 15 mice). **d**, Left, schematic showing the generalized linear model (GLM) used to predict neural activity from behavior; Right, example fit of selected neurons with cvR² (0.50 and 0.01). **e**, Distribution of cvR² across all mice for GLMs trained using only behavior (left, N = 15 mice, mean: 0.08) and **f,** using behavior with cell coupling (right, N = 15 mice, mean:

0.46). **g,** Predicted cell coupling (relative strength of connectivity) between neurons in one example mouse. See also Extended Data Fig. 3.

Fig. 3 Population dynamics in female VMHvl during mating.

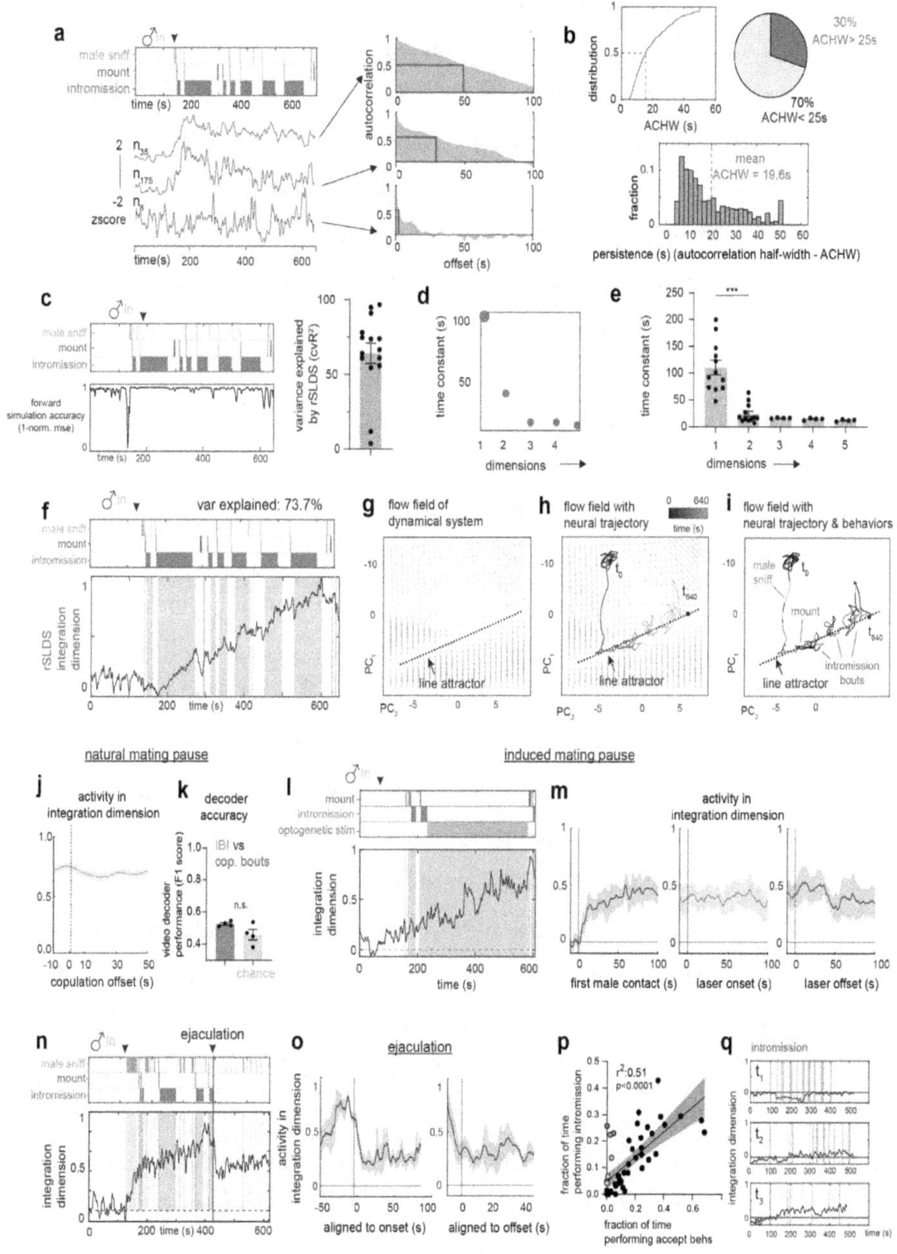

Figure 3 | An approximate line attractor in female VMHvl during mating.

a, Left, example VMHvl neurons in female showing a range of persistent activity (zscored $\Delta F/F$); Right, auto-correlation half-width (ACHW) as a measure of persistent activity, for example units shown. **b,** Left, cumulative distribution of ACHW for all units; Right, distribution of the number of neurons with ACHW > 25s (N = 4 mice). **c,** Left, rSLDS model performance measured by forward simulation accuracy (calculated as [1-normalized mean squared error, mse])[91] in an example mouse. Right, variance explained by rSLDS model fit without an input term (see Methods) for all mice (N = 15 mice, mean = 64.08%). The variance explained by the two outliers can be increased by incorporating an input term. **d,** Time constants reveal a single dimension with a large time constant. **e,** Distribution of time constants across animals fit by the rSLDS. Time constants sorted by magnitude in each animal (N = 15 mice). **f,** Dynamics of the integration dimension reveals a ramping dimension, aligned to male mating behaviors in an example trial. **g,** Flow field of VMHvl α dynamical system colored by rSLDS states. **h,** Flow field of VMHvl α dynamical system showing neural trajectories in state space. **i,** Neural state space of VMHvl α dynamical system highlighting regions where fixed points are present (dash line). **j,** Behavior triggered average of the normalized activity of the integration dimension aligned to the offset of male copulation. **k,** Videoframe behavioral decoder performance trained on neural data from copulation bouts vs. inter-bout intervals. **l,** Dynamics of the integration dimension in an example female combined with optogenetic inhibition of mating behaviors in the interacting male. **m,** Behavior triggered average of the normalized activity of the integration dimension aligned to first male contact (left), optogenetic mating inhibition onset (middle) and inhibition offset (right) (N = 4 mice). **n,** Dynamics of the integration dimension, aligned to male mating behaviors in an example trial with ejaculation. **o,** Behavior triggered average of the normalized activity of the integration dimension aligned to the ejaculation onset and offset (N=4 mice). **p,** Scatter plots of time spent performing intromission and time spent performing accept behaviors to identify trials with high intromission and low receptivity (colored dots). **q,** Example traces of the integration dimension for trials with intromission but low receptivity (identified from **p**).

Fig. 4 Line attractor dynamics encodes female sexual receptivity across days.

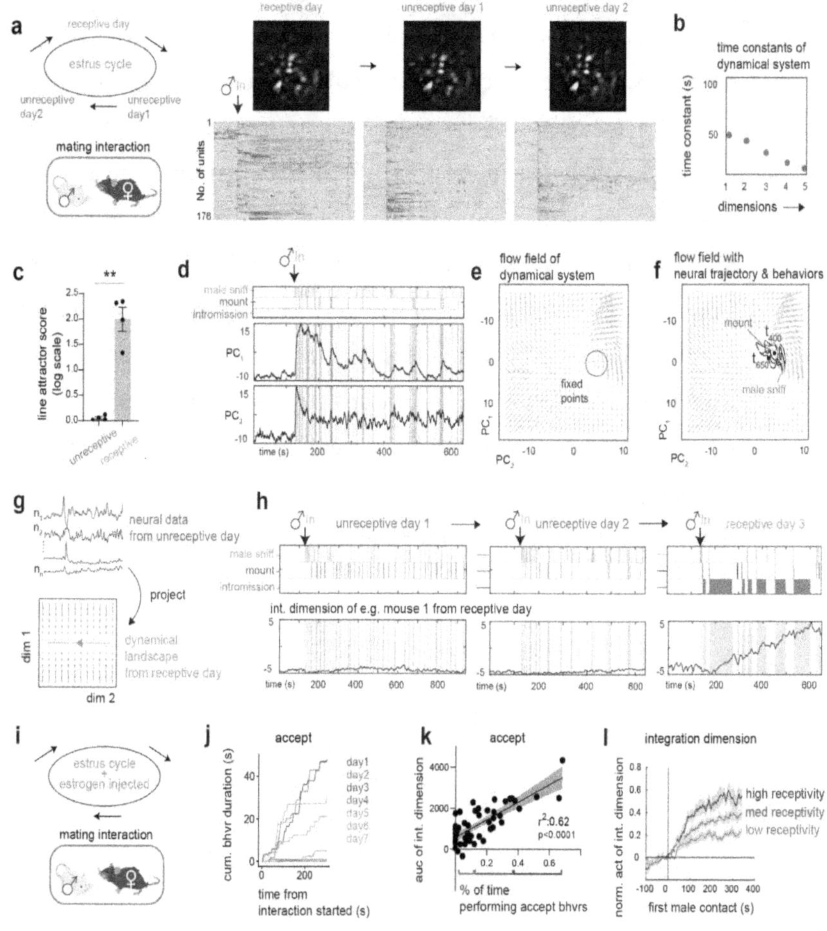

Figure 4| Line attractor dynamics encoded female sexual receptivity across days.

a, Left, illustration for longitudinal imaging strategy across estrus states of naturally cycling females; Right, example longitudinal imaging planes and traces from one female. Units were sorted by temporal correlation. Color scale indicates z-scored activity. **b,** Time constants of VMHvl α dynamical system on one unreceptive day. **c,** Line attractor scores for dynamical systems fit during receptive and unreceptive days (N = 4 mice). **d,** Low dimensional principal components of VMHvl α rSLDS fit model on unreceptive day.

Principal components show fast time locked dynamics and lack ramping and persistence. **e,** Flow field of VMHvl α dynamical system on unreceptive day. **f,** Same as **e**, showing neural trajectories in state space colored by time and behaviors. **g,** Schematic illustrating the projection of neural activity from an unreceptive day into fit dynamical system from a receptive day. **h,** Dynamics of integration dimension in VMHvl discovered during a receptive day (same example trial as shown in Fig. 3f) compared to activity of the same dimension on unreceptive days. **i,** Illustration for longitudinal imaging strategy across estrus states of naturally cycling females with estrogen injection. **j,** Accepting behaviors displayed in mating interactions across days from one example female. **k,** The scatter plots of the integration dimension values and the amount of female accepting behaviors (linear regression, $R^2=0.62$) in each trials. **l,** The integration dimension activity aligned to the first male contact, in high, medium or low receptivity trials, defined in **k.** ****p<0.0001, Wilcoxon matched-pairs signed rank test.

Supplementary figures

Extended Data Fig.1 Additional information for Fig. 1.

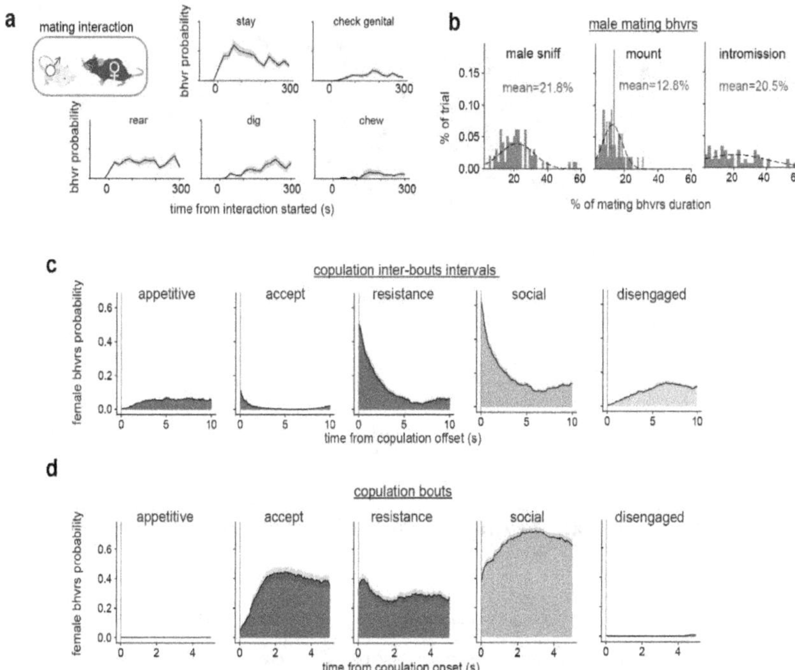

Extended Data Figure 1. | Additional information for Fig. 1.

a, The probability of female behaviors every 20s (n=74 trials, N=28 mice). **b,** Distribution of the percentage of time males displayed mating behaviors in each trial (n=74 trials). **c,** The probability of female behaviors aligned to male copulation offsets and **d,** copulation onsets.

Extended Data Fig.2 Neural responses to conspecific sex, additional inforamtion for Fig. 2.

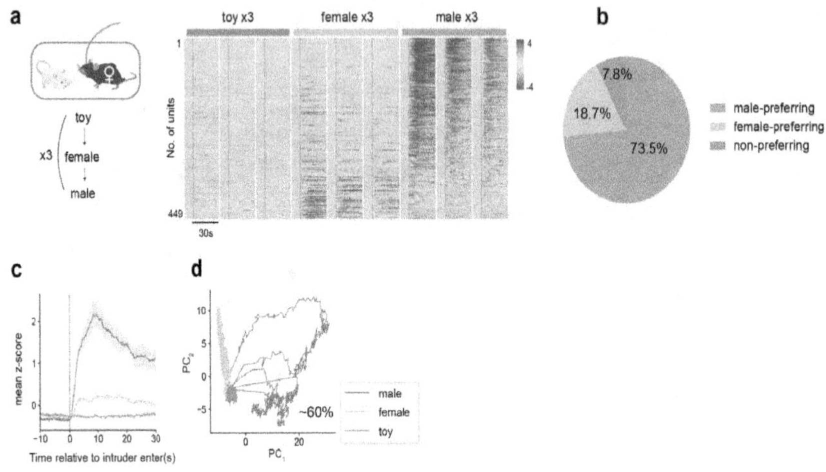

Extended Data Figure 2. | Neural responses to conspecific sex, additional information for Figure 2.

a, Left, diagram of sex representation test. Each intruder was presented for 1 min. Right, concatenated average responses to toy, female, or male (N = 8 mice). Color scale indicates z-scored activity. Units were sorted by temporal correlation. **b,** Percentages of male- or female-preferring cells (calculated by Choice Probability). **c,** Mean responses of female VMHvl$_{Esr1}$ α cells to male, female and toy (N=8 mice). **d,** PCA of neuronal responses to male, female and toy from one example female.

Extended Data Fig.3 Additional information for Fig. 2.

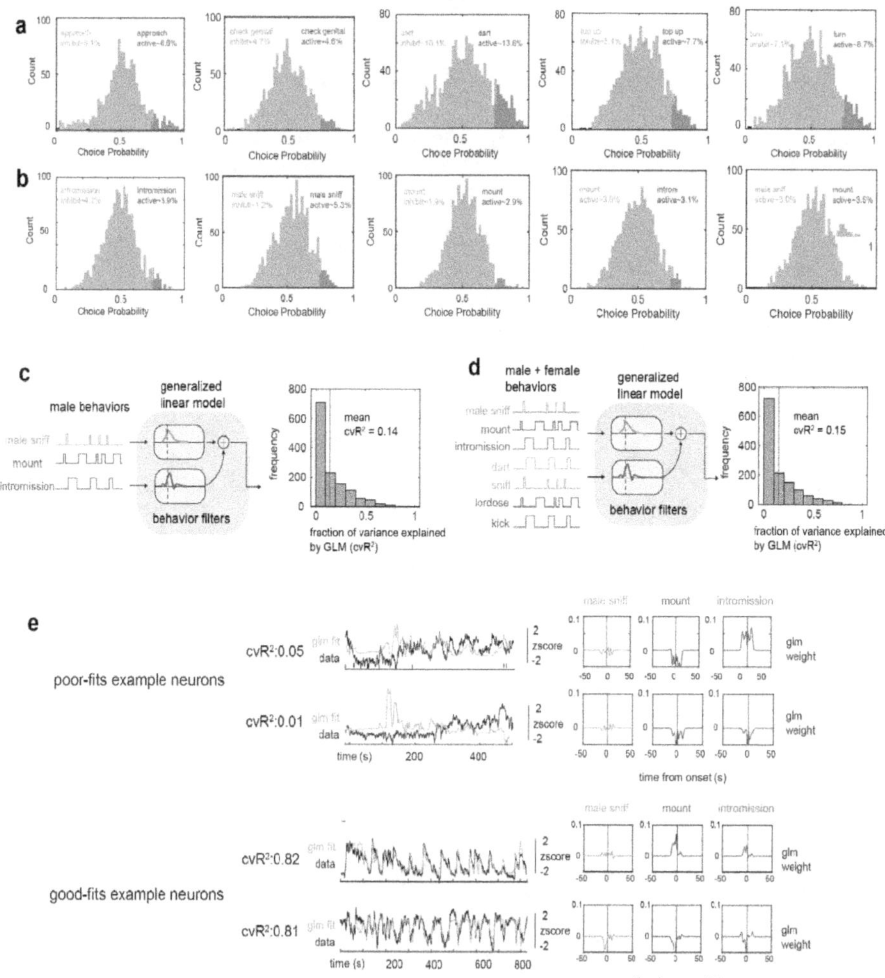

Extended Data Figure 3. | Additional information for Fig. 2.

a, Choice Probability (CP) histograms and percentages of tuned cells for female behaviors.

cutoff: CP>0.7 or <0.3 and >2σ. N = 15 mice. **b,** Same as **a**, but for male behavior. **c**, Schematic showing generalized linear model (GLM) used to predict neural activity from male behaviors and distribution of cvR² across all mice, or **d,** both male and female behaviors and distribution of cvR² across all mice (N = 15 mice). **e,** Example generalized linear model fits and behavior filters for poorly and well fit neurons. **f**, GLM using both behavior and coupling to predict activity in single neurons. **g**, Predicted cell coupling between neurons in example mice.

Extended Data Fig.4 Decoder analysis, additional information for Fig. 2.

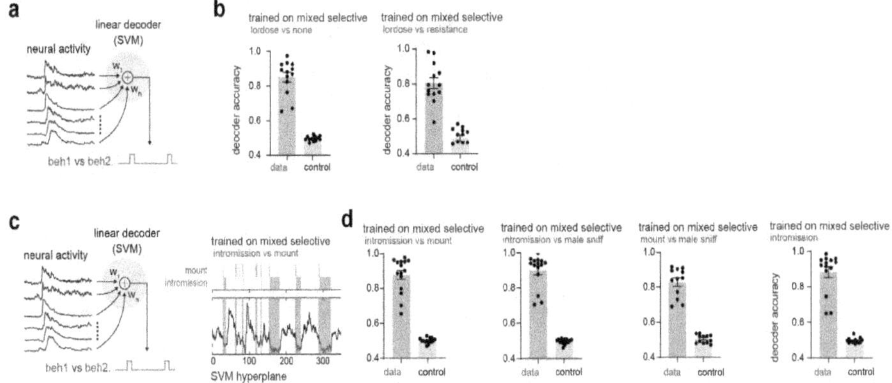

Extended Data Figure 4. | Decoder analysis, additional information for Fig. 2.

a, schematic showing linear support vector machine (SVM) decoder trained on frames of male mating behaviors. **b**, , performance of the decoder trained to separate female behavior. Left, performance of decoder trained to separate frames of lordosis versus all remaining frames. Right, performance of decoder trained to separate frames of lordosis versus resistance behaviors. **c**, Same as a, but showing the decoder hyperplane for separating male behaviors (mount versus intromission) on right. (***p<0.001). (N = 15 mice). **d**, performance of decoders trained to separate intromission versus mount, intromission versus male sniffing, mount versus male sniffing and intromission versus remaining frames male sniffing, mount versus male sniffing and intromission versus remaining frames (***p<0.001, N = 15 mice).

Extended Data Fig.5 Additional example trials with rSLDS model fit, additional information for Fig. 3

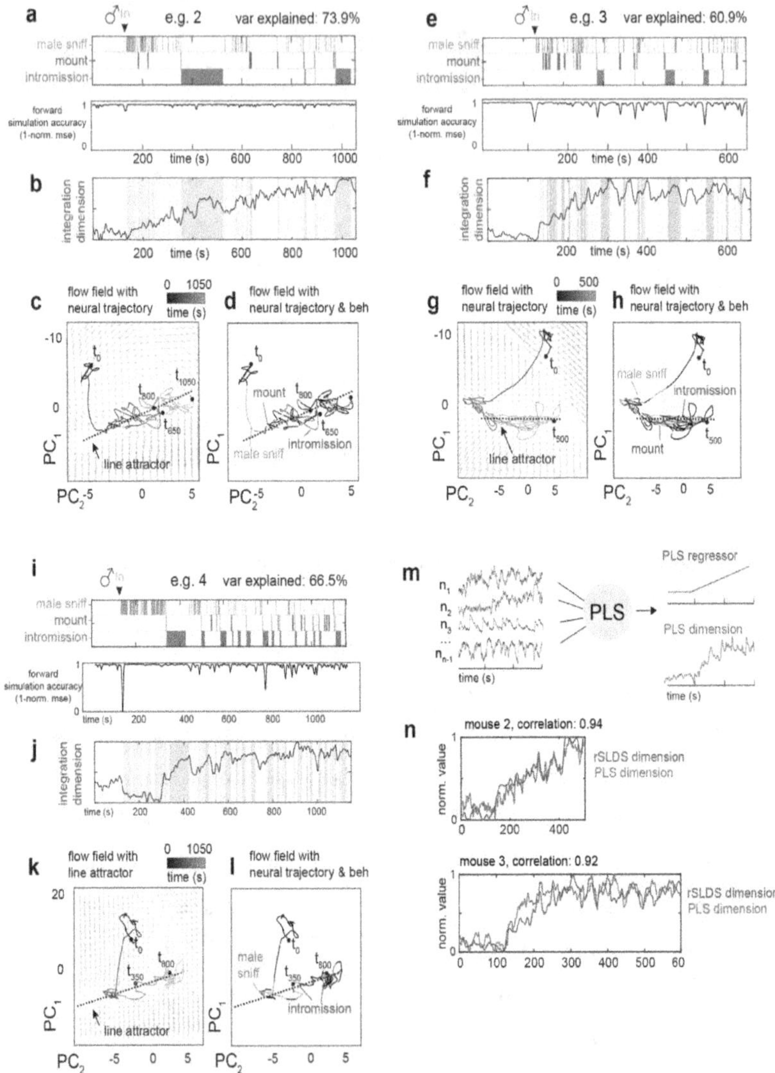

Extended Data Figure 5. | Additional example trials with rSLDS model fit, additional information for Fig. 3.

a, Recurrent switching linear dynamical systems (rSLDS) model fit forward simulation accuracy aligned to male behaviors in example trial 2. **b,** Dynamics of the integration dimension in trial 2. **c,** Flow field of VMHvl α dynamical system showing neural trajectories in state space, annotated by time from male encounter

(t_0) for trial 2. **d,** Neural state space of VMHvl α dynamical system highlighting behaviors and the region containing the line attractor for trial 2. **ef,** the same as **a-d** for example trial 3. **i-k,** the same as **b-e** for example trial 4. **m,** Schematic illustrating partial least squares regression to extract integration dynamics in VMHvl. **n,** Comparison of rSLDS integration dimension and PLS dimension for two example mice showing a high correlation.

Extended Data Fig.6 Dynamics of single cell activity, additional inforamtion for Fig. 3.

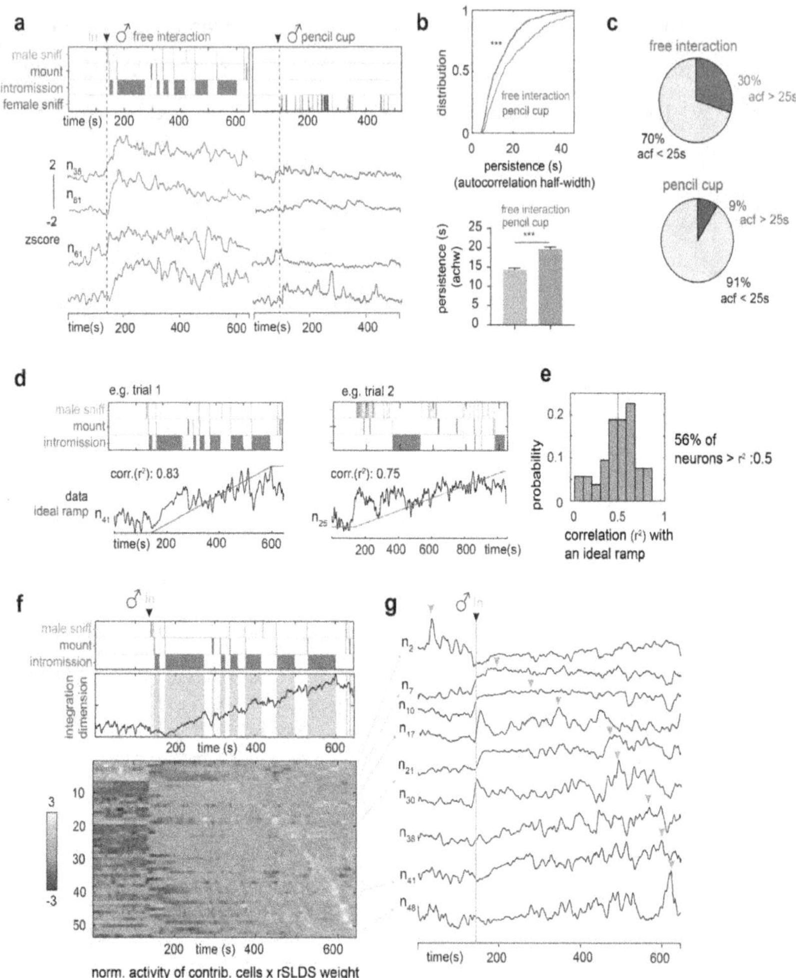

Extended Data Figure 6. | Dynamics of single cell activity, additional information for Fig. 3.

a, Dynamics of persistently active neurons identified during receptive interaction with pencil-cup assay. **b,** Cumulative distribution of ACHW for same neurons during free interaction vs pencil cup assay ***p<0.001. **c,** Pie chart indicating fraction of neurons with ACHW > 25s in free interaction and in pencil cup assay. **d,** Correlation of example unit activity with an ideal ramp. **e,** Distribution of correlation of individual neuron activity with ideal ramp. **f,** *Upper*, relationship of male behavior to weighted average of all units contributing to integration dimension as a function of time. Data from the same example trial as shown in Fig. 3f. *Lower*, normalized activity (z-score) of individual units times rSLDS weight for each unit exhibiting a significant weight in the integration dimension, sorted by time to peak. **g,** Traces of example units from **f**, *lower*. Yellow arrow indicates peak of activity for each unit.

Extended Data Fig.7 Single cell activity patterns at receptive and unreceptive states, additional information for Fig. 4.

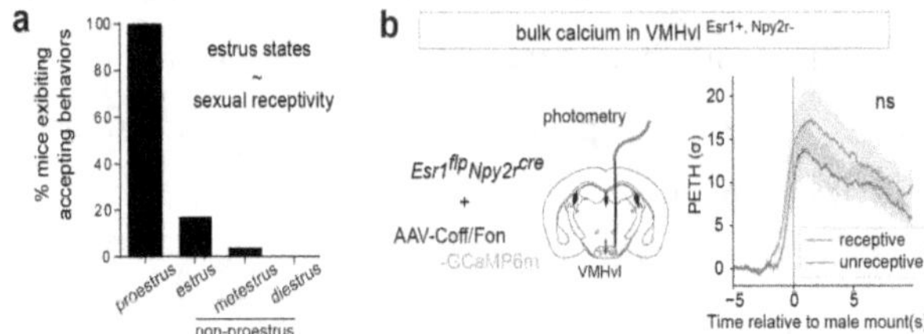

Extended Data Figure 7. | Single cell activity patterns at receptive and unreceptive states, additional information for Fig. 4.

a, Correlation between female estrus states and the presence of sexual receptivity, measured by whether female displayed accepting behaviors during interaction with male. **b,** Photometry recording in female VMHvl α cells during receptive and unreceptive mating interactions.

Extended Data Fig.8 Population dynamics at receptive and unreceptive states, addtional information for Fig. 4.

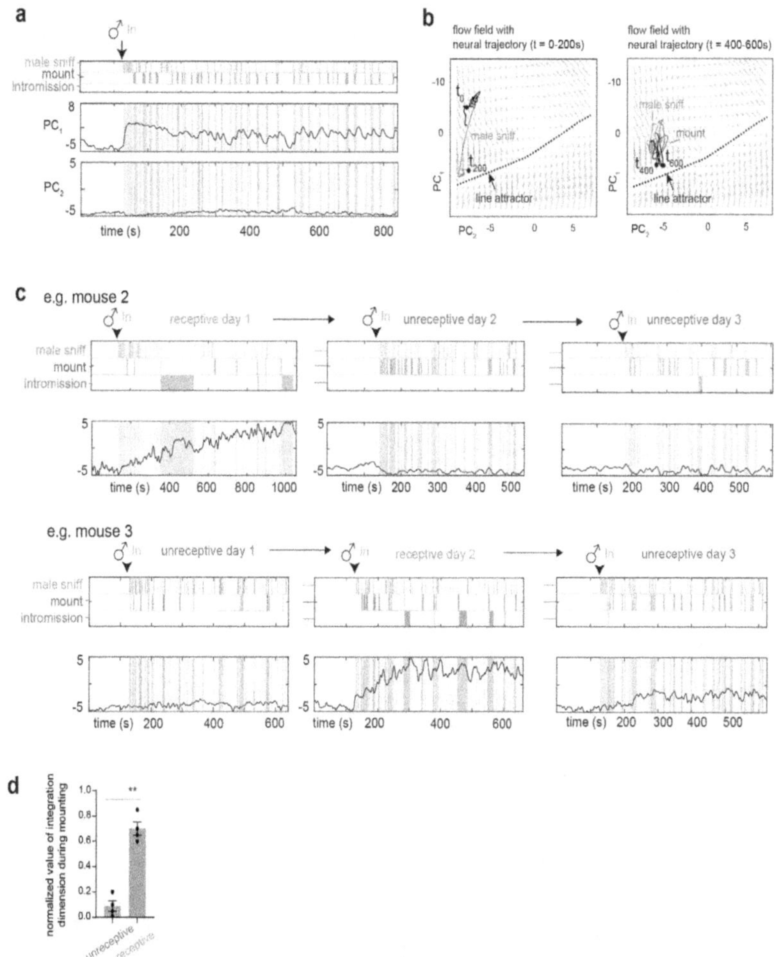

Extended Data Figure 8. | Population dynamics during receptive and unreceptive days, additional information for Fig. 4.

a, Low dimensional principal components of VMHvl α dynamical system in receptive day with neural data projected from unreceptive day. **b,** Flow field of VMHvl α dynamical system in receptive day with neural trajectories projected from unreceptive for $t = 0$ to $t = 200s$ (left) and $t = 200s$ to $t = 400s$ (right). **c,** Dynamics of integration dimension in two more example mice discovered during receptive day compared to activity of the same dimension on unreceptive days. **d,** Quantification of normalized value of integration dimension during male-mounting in unreceptive and receptive days.

Extended Data Fig.9 Single cell persistence at receptive and unreceptive states, additional information for Fig. 4.

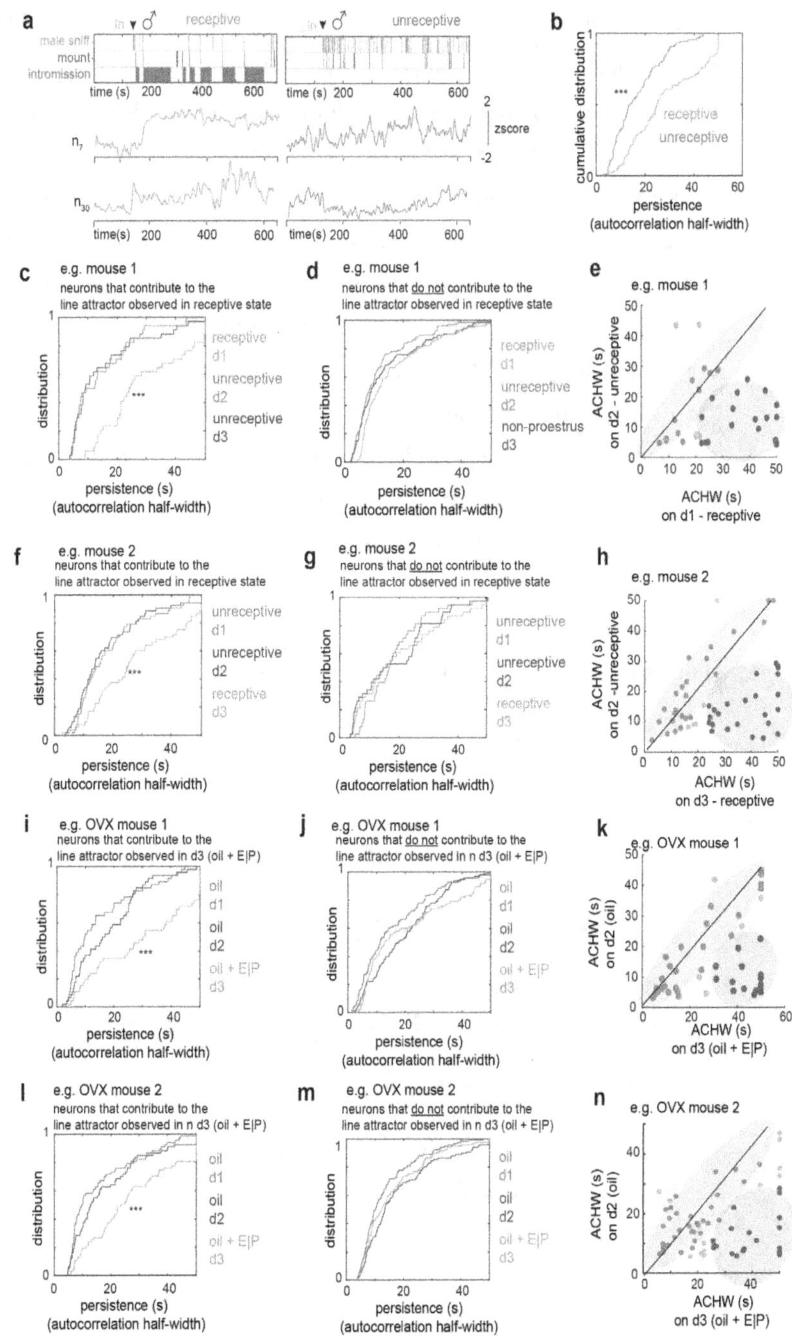

additional information for Fig. 4.

a, Example units active during both receptive (red traces, left) and unreceptive (blue traces, right), showing persistence on receptive day and fast dynamics on the unreceptive days. **b,** Comparison of cumulative distribution of ACHWs to that of same neurons on unreceptive days. Data from example mouse 1. **c,** Cumulative distribution of ACHWs for units with significant weights on integration dimension across receptive and unreceptive day. Data from example mouse 1. **d,** Cumulative distribution of ACHWs for example mouse 1, for units that do not contribute to the integration dimension on the receptive day, compared on receptive vs unreceptive days. **e,** Scatter plot of ACHWs for units with significant weights on integration dimension for receptive day vs unreceptive day. Data from example mouse 1. (**f-h**) Same as **c-e** for example mouse 2. **i,** Cumulative distribution of ACHWs for units with significant weights on integration dimension across hormone primed (day 3) and non-primed days (days 2, 1). Data from example OVX mouse 1. **j,** Cumulative distribution of AHWs for example OVX mouse 1, for units that do not contribute to the integration dimension across hormone primed (day 3) and non-primed days (days 2, 1). **k,** Scatter plot of ACHWs for units with significant weights on integration dimension for hormoneprimed day vs non-primed day. Data from example OVX mouse 1 (**l-n**) Same as **i-j**. for example OVX mouse 2.

Extended Data Fig.10 Population dynamics before and after OVX in the same female, additional information for Fig. 4.

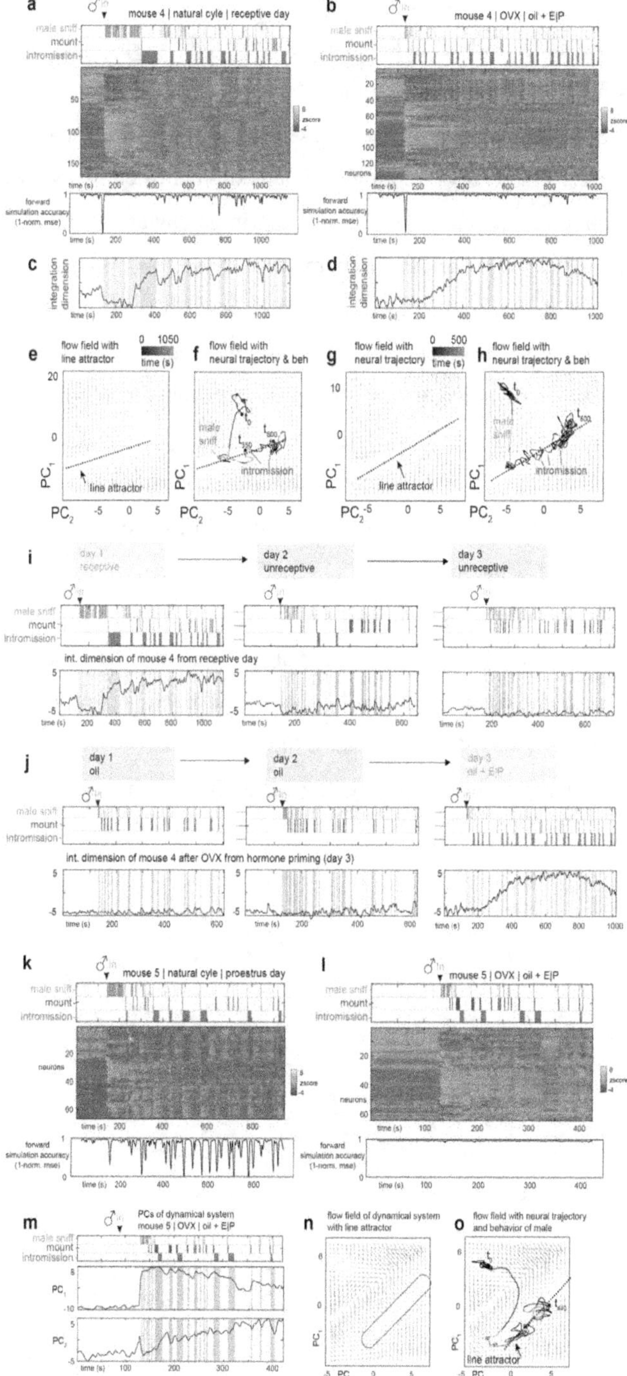

Extended Data Figure 10. | Population dynamics before and after OVX in the same female, additional information for Fig. 4.

(**a, b,**) Neural raster and behaviors and rSLDS model performance (measured as forward simulation error, see Methods) for one example mouse in receptive day of natural estrus cycle **a,** and same mouse on hormone primed day after OVX (day3, oil + E|P) **b. (c, d,)** Integration dimension identified by rSLDS on natural cycle receptive day **c,** and during hormone primed day after OVX **d. (e, f,)** Flow field **e,** and neural trajectories of dynamical system **f,** with line attractor highlighted of model fit during the receptive state of the estrus cycle. (**g, h,**) Same as **e, f,** for model fit during hormone primed day after OVX. **i,** Dynamics of integration dimension discovered during natural cycle receptive day compared to activity of the same dimension on unreceptive days. **j,** Dynamics of integration dimension in the same mouse discovered during hormone primed day (day 3) compared to the activity of the same dimension during non-primed days. (**k, l,**) Neural raster and behaviors and rSLDS model performance for mouse in proestrus day of natural estrus cycle **k,** and same mouse on hormone primed day after OVX (day3, oil + E|P) **l. m,** Principal components of mouse dynamic system fit during hormone primed day. (**n, o,**) Flow field **n,** and neural trajectories of dynamical system. **o,** with line attractor highlighted of model fit during the hormone primed day after OVX in mouse.

Extended Data Fig.11 Additional information for Fig. 4.

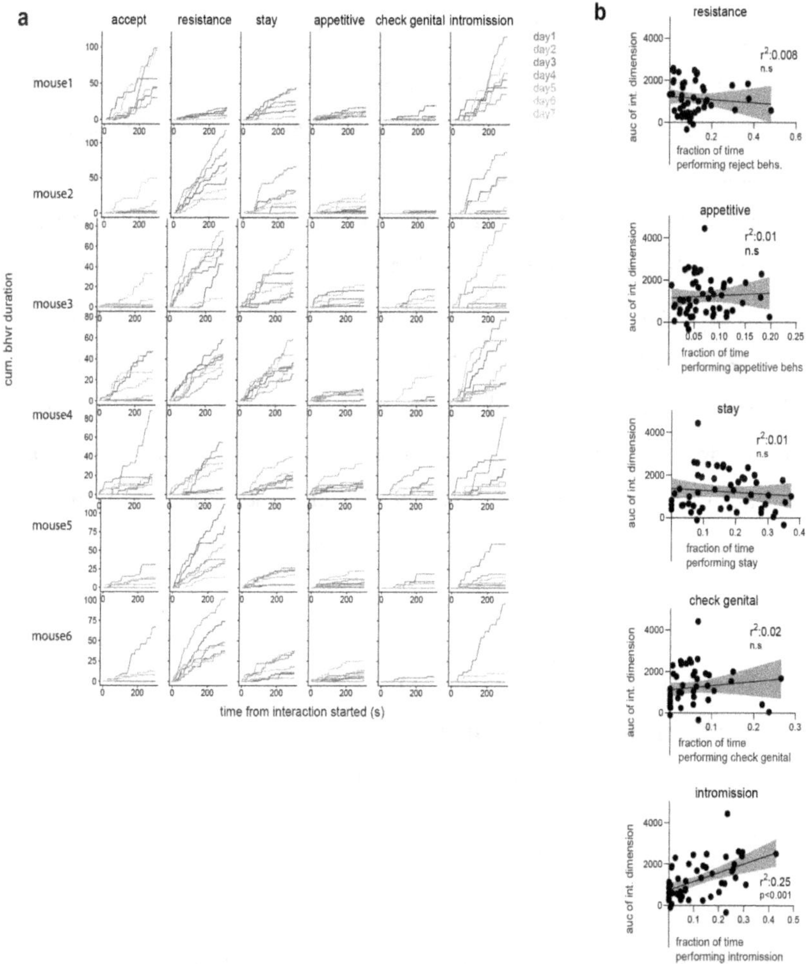

Extended Data Figure 11. | Additional information for Fig. 4.

a, Behaviors displayed in mating interactions across days from all the recorded females. **b,** The scatter plots of the integration dimension values and the amount of female resistance behaviors (linear regression, $R^2 = 0.008$), appetitive behaviors ($R^2 = 0.01$), staying ($R^2 = 0.01$), checking genital ($R^2 = 0.02$) and male intromission ($R^2 = 0.25$).

Materials and methods

Mice

All experimental procedures involving the use of live mice or their tissues were carried out in accordance with NIH guidelines and approved by the Institute Animal Care and Use Committee (IACUC) and the Institute Biosafety Committee (IBC) at the California Institute of Technology (Caltech). All mice in this study, including wild-type and transgenic mice, were bred at Caltech or purchased from Charles River Laboratory. Group housed C57BL/6N female or singly housed male mice (2-5 months) were used as experimental mice. *Npy2r^cre^* mice (Jackson Laboratory stock no. 029285) (=N1), *Esr1^cre^* mice, *Esr1^flp^* mice (>N10), *Sf1^cre^* mice (Jackson Laboratory stock no. 012462) were backcrossed into the C57BL/6N background and bred at Caltech. Heterozygous *Npy2r^cre^*, *Esr1^cre^* or double heterozygote *Esr1^flp/+^Npy2r^cre/+^* mice were used for cell-specific targeting experiments and were genotyped by PCR analysis using genomic DNA from tail tissue. All mice were housed in ventilated micro-isolator cages in a temperature-controlled environment (median temperature 23°C, humidity 60%), under a reversed 11-h dark–13-h light cycle, with ad libitum access to food and water. Mouse cages were changed weekly.

Surgeries

Surgeries were performed on female Esr1^Flp/+^Npy2r ^Cre/+^ females aged 2 months. Virus injection and implantation were performed as described previously[4,25]. Briefly, animals were anaesthetized with isoflurane (5% for induction and 1.5% for maintenance) and placed on a stereotaxic frame (David Kopf Instruments). Virus was injected into the target area using a pulled-glass capillary (World Precision Instruments) and a pressure injector (Micro4 controller, World Precision Instruments), at a flow rate of 20 nl min^{-1}. The glass capillary was left in place for 10 min following injection before withdrawal. Lenses were slowly lowered into the brain and fixed to the skull with dental cement (Metabond, Parkell). Females were co-housed with a vasectomized male mouse after virus injection and lens implantation. Four weeks after lens implantation, mice were head-fixed on a running wheel and a miniaturized micro-endoscope (nVista, Inscopix) was lowered over the implanted lens until GCaMP-expressing fluorescent neurons were in focus. Once GCaMP-expressing neurons were detected, a permanent baseplate was attached to the skull with dental cement.

The co-housed vasectomized males were removed.

Virus injection and GRIN lens implantation

The following AAVs were used in this study, with injection titers as indicated. Viruses with a high original titer were diluted with clean PBS on the day of use. AAV-DJ-EF1a-Coff/FonGCaMP6m ($4.5e^{12}$, Addgene plasmid) was packaged at the HHMI Janelia Research Campus virus facility. "Coff/Fon" indicates Cre-OFF/FLP-ON virus. Stereotaxic injection coordinates were based on the Paxinos and Franklin atlas. Virus injection: VMHvl, AP: -1.6, ML: ±0.78, DV: -5.73; GRIN lens implantation: VMHvl: AP: -1.6, ML: -0.75, DV: -5.6 ($\varnothing0.6 \times 7.3$ mm GRIN lens).

Vaginal cytology

To determine the estrus phases of tested females, vaginal smear cytology was applied on the same day as the behavior test. A vaginal smear was collected immediately after the behavioral test and stained with 0.1% crystal violet solution for 1 minute. Cell types in the stained vaginal smear were checked microscopically. In this study, the proestrus phase was characterized by many nucleated epithelial, some cornified epithelial and no leukocytes.

Hormone priming

Female mice were ovariectomized and estrus was induced by hormone priming. Estradiol benzoate (E2) and progesterone (PG) powder was dissolved in sesame oil. For primed females, 50ul 200ng/ml E2 was delivered subcutaneously on day-2 and day-1 at 3pm. 10mg/ml PG was delivered subcutaneously on the day of test at 10am. Behavior test was performed 4-6 hours after PG injection. For unprimed female, sesame oil was injected at the same time points as hormone injections. Vaginal smear cytology was applied on the same day as the behavior test to make sure that the females were completely primed or unprimed. For estrogen-injected females used in Fig. 3 and Fig. 4, 50ul 200ng/ml E2 was delivered subcutaneously everyday at 10am. Behavior tests were conducted after the first two days of injection.

Sex representation assay

All behavior tests were performed under red light. Group housed C57BL/6N male and female mice (2-4 months) were used for the test. Tested female was acclimated in her home cage under the recording setup[79] for 10 minutes. A toy, a female or a male was introduced to the tested female with a 90-second interval. Each interaction lasted for 1 minute before transitioning into the consummatory phase. The sequential representations were repeated for 3 times.

Mating assay

Singly housed sexually experienced C57BL/6N male were used for mating assay. Male mice used for test were initially co-housed with a female mouse for at least 1 week and singly housed at least 1 week before test. On the day of test. Male mouse was acclimated in his home cage under the recording setup. A random female mouse was placed into male cage until three male mounting bouts were observed. The tested female mice were acclimated in a new cage for 10 minutes before being introduced into the male cage. The male contact mating interaction lasted for 5-15 mins. At the end of the free interaction, a pencil cup was introduced to restrain the male. Then the imaging and behavior recording during the noncontact period continued for 3-5 mins.

Wireless optogenetic male mating inhibition assay

Singly housed sexually experienced Sf1-Cre[+/-] males were used in this test. All hardware and wireless devices for optogenetic stimulation were sourced from NeuroLux (Urbana, IL). Specifically, AAV2-EF1a-DIO-hChR2(H134R)-EYFP-WPRE-pA (4.2e[12], UNC vector core) was unilaterally injected into ventromedial hypothalamus (VMHdm) of the male mice at coordinates: AP: −1.5, ML: +0.4, DV: −5.6. Simultaneously, wireless optogenetic devices were implanted. A recovery period of three weeks followed the surgical procedures to allow for optimal viral vector expression and ensure the animals' well-being. Subsequently, a mating assay was performed, and when multiple successful copulations were observed, male mice were exposed to a wirelessly powered blue light photostimulation (473 nm, 1-5 minutes, 20Hz, 10W). During the stimulation, male mice promptly discontinued all matingrelated behaviors, including vocalization, sniffing, mounting or intromission, instead exhibiting exploratory behaviors within the homecage and distancing themselves from the female mouse. Following the cessation of photostimulation, male mice typically resumed mating-related behaviors, either immediately or with a delay.

Behavior annotations

Behavior videos were manually annotated using a custom MATLAB-based behavior annotation interface. A 'baseline' period of 2 min when the animal was alone in its cage was recorded at the start of every recording session.

During female-male interaction, we manually annotated the following male mating behaviors: male sniff, mount, intromission and ejaculation.

For the same video, we annotated the following female mating behaviors: approach, sniff, lordose, wiggle, stay, dart, top up, kick, turn, check genital. 'Approach': Female faced male and walked to it without pausing. 'Sniff': Female actively sniffed male. 'Lordose': Female abdomen was on the ground and motionless or showing an arched back posture responding to male mounting or intromission. 'Wiggle': Female continuously moving her head or body responding to male mounting or intromission. 'Stay': Female quietly stayed in place, but abdomen was not clearly on the ground, responding to male mounting or intromission. 'Dart': Female quickly ran away from male, responding to male mating behaviors. 'Top up': Female stood up to conceal the anogenital area, responding to male mating behaviors. 'Kick': Female kicked the male, responding to male mating behaviors. 'Turn': Female turned away from male, responding to mating mounting or intromission. 'Check genital': Female examined her genital area, usually after male mounting or intromission.

'Lordose', 'wiggle', 'stay', dart', 'top up', 'kick' and 'turn' were grouped as responsive mating behaviors. 'Approach', 'sniff' and 'check genital' were grouped as female selfinitiated mating behaviors.

'Approach' and 'sniff' were grouped as appetitive mating behaviors. 'Lordose' and 'wiggle' were grouped as accepting mating behaviors. 'Dart', 'top up', 'kick' and 'turn' were grouped as resistance mating behaviors.

All appetitive, accepting and resistance behaviors were grouped as social behaviors.

For the same video, we also annotated the following female non-social disengaged behaviors: rear, dig, chew. 'Rear': Female extended her body upright and attempted to explore outside the testing chamber. 'Dig': Female dig beddings. 'Chew': Female stood up and chew with her mouth.

Fiber photometry

The fiber photometry setup was as previously described in earlier research with minor modifications. We used 470 nm LEDs (M470F3, Thorlabs, filtered with 470-10 nm bandpass filters FB470-10, Thorlabs) for fluorophore excitation, and 405 nm LEDs for isosbestic excitation (M405FP1, Thorlabs, filtered with 410–10 nm bandpass filters FB410-10, Thorlabs). LEDs were modulated at 208 Hz (470 nm) and 333 Hz (405 nm) and controlled by a real-time processor (RZ5P, Tucker David Technologies) via an LED driver (DC4104, Thorlabs). The emission signal from the 470 nm excitation was normalized to the emission signal from the isosbestic excitation (405 nm), to control for motion artefacts, photobleaching and levels of GCaMP6m expression. LEDs were coupled to a 425 nm longpass dichroic mirror (Thorlabs, DMLP425R) via fiber optic patch cables (diameter 400 mm, N.A., 0.48; Doric lenses). Emitted light was collected via the patch cable, coupled to a 490 nm longpass dichroic mirror (DMLP490R, Thorlabs), filtered (FF01-542/27-25, Sem- rock), collimated through a focusing lens (F671SMA-405, Thorlabs) and detected by the photodetectors (Model 2151, Newport). Recordings were acquired using Synapse software (Tucker Davis Technologies). On the test day, after at least 5 minutes of acclimation under the recording setup, the female was first recorded for 5 minutes to establish a baseline. Then behavior assays were proceeded and fluorescence were recorded for the indicated period of time, as described in the text. All data analyses were performed in Python. Behavioral video files and fiber photometry data were time-locked. Fn was calculated using normalized (405 nm) fluorescence signals from 470 nm excitation. $Fn(t) = 100 \times [F470(t) - F405fit(t)] / F405fit(t)$. For the peri-event time histogram (PETH), the baseline value F_0 and standard deviation SD_0. was calculated using a -5 to -3 second window. Overlapping behavioral bouts within this time window were excluded from the analysis. Then PETH was calculated by $[(Fn(t) - F_0]/ SD_0$.

Micro-endoscopic imaging data Acquisition

Imaging data were acquired at 30 Hz with $2\times$ spatial downsampling; light-emitting diode power (0.2–0.5) and gain (1–$8\times$) were adjusted depending on the brightness of GCaMP expression as determined by the image histogram according to the user manual. A transistor– transistor logic (TTL) pulse from the Sync port of the data acquisition box (DAQ, Inscopix) was used for synchronous triggering of StreamPix7 (Norpix) for video recording.

Micro-endoscopic data extraction and preprocessing.

Miniscope data were acquired at 30 Hz using the Inscopix Data Acquisition Software as $2\times$ down sampled .isxd files. Preprocessing and motion correction were performed using Inscopix Data Processing Software. Briefly, raw imaging data from three recording dates were concatenated. $2\times$ spatially down sampled, motion corrected and temporally down sampled to 10 Hz. Further and exported as a .tiff image stack. A spatial band-pass filter was then applied to remove out-of-focus background. After preprocessing, calcium traces were extracted and deconvolved using the CNMF-E large data pipeline with the following parameters: patch_dims = [32, 32], gSig = 3, gSiz = 13, ring_radius

= 19, min_corr = 0.72, min_pnr = 8. The spatial and temporal components of every extracted unit were carefully inspected manually (SNR, PNR, size, motion artefacts, decay kinetics and so on) and outliers (obvious deviations from the normal distribution) were discarded. The extracted traces were then z-scored before analysis.

Longitudinal imaging data extraction and preprocessing.
The females performed mating assay and were imaged for consecutive 3-7 days. 'Receptive day' was defined as female displayed accepting behaviors on the testing day, while 'unreceptive day' was defined as female did not display accepting behaviors on the testing day. Miniscope data from one receptive day and two unreceptive days were selected and concatenated to one .isxd file. Data was preprocessed and the traces were extracted as described in the last section. The three-day concatenated traces were z-scored, and then split to multiple traces for individual days.

Choice probability
Choice probability is a metric that estimates how well either of two different behaviors can be predicted/distinguished, based on the activity of any given neuron during these two behaviors. CP of single neurons was computed using previously described methods[25]. To compute the CP of a single neuron for any behavior pair, 1 s binned neuronal responses occurring during each of the two behaviors were used to generate a receiver operating characteristic curve. CP is defined as the area under the curve bounded between 0 and 1. A CP of 0.5 indicates that the activity of the neuron cannot distinguish between the two alternative behaviors. We defined a neuron as being capable of distinguishing between two behaviors if the CP of that neuron was >0.7 or <0.3 and was >2 σ or <−2 σ of the CP computed using shuffled data (repeated 1000 times).

Generalized linear model

To predict neural activity from behavior, we trained generalized linear models to predict the activity of each neurons k, as a weighted linear combination of 3 male behaviors: male sniffing, mounting and intromission as follows:

$$y_!(t) = x^\sim(t)\beta^\sim + \varphi$$

Here, $y_!(t)$ is the calcium activity of neuron k at time t, $x^\sim(t)$ is a feature vector of 3 binary male behaviors at time lags ranging from t-D to t where D = 10s. $\beta^\sim$ is a behavior-filter which described how a neuron integrates stimulus over a 10s period (example filters are shown in Extended Data Fig.1d-e). φ is an error term. The model was fit using 10-fold cross validation with ridge regularization and model performance is reported as cross-validated $R^"$ (cv$R^"$). To account for cell-cell interactions within the network, we also used the activity of simultaneously imaged neurons as regressors in addition to behavior as previously performed[92,93].

Dynamical system modelling

Recurrent-switching linear dynamical system (rSLDS) models[89,99] are fit to neural data as previously described[91]. Briefly, rSLDS is a generative state-space model that decomposes non-linear time series data into a set of linear dynamical systems, also called 'states'. The model describes three sets of variables: a set of discrete states (z), a set of latent factors (x) that captures the low-dimensional nature of neural activity, and the activity of recorded neurons (y). While the model can also allow for the incorporation of external inputs based on behavior features, such external inputs were not included in our first analysis.

The model is formulated as follows: At each timepoint, there is a discrete state $z_\# \in \{1, \dots, K\}$ that depends recurrently on the continuous latent factors (x) as follows:

$$(z_{\#\$\%} \mid z_\# = k, x_\#) = \text{softmax}\{R_!x_\# + r_!\} \tag{1}$$

where $R_! \in \mathbb{R}^{\&\times\&}$ and $r_! \in \mathbb{R}^{\&}$ parameterizes a map from the previous discrete state and continuous state to a distribution over the next discrete states using a softmax link function. The discrete state $z_\#$ determines the linear dynamical system used to generate the latent factors at any time t:

$$x_\# = A_{(!}x_\#)\% + b_{(!} + \epsilon_\# \tag{2}$$

where $A_! \in \mathbb{R}^{*\times*}$ is a dynamics matrix and $b_! \in \mathbb{R}^+$ is a bias vector, where D is the dimensionality of the latent space and $\epsilon_\# \sim (0, Q_{(!)})$ is a Gaussian-distributed noise (aka innovation) term.

Lastly, we can recover the activity of recorded neurons by modelling activity as a linear noisy Gaussian observation $y_\# \in \mathbb{R}^{\cdot}$ where N is the number of recorded neurons:

$$y_\# = Cx_\# + d + \delta_\# \tag{3}$$

For $C \in \mathbb{R}^{\cdot\times+}$ and $\delta_\# \sim N(0, S)$, a Gaussian noise term. Overall, the system parameters that rSLDS needs to learn consists of the state transition dynamics, library of linear dynamical system matrices and neuron-specific emission parameters, which we write as:

$$\theta = \{\{A_!b_!, Q_!, R_!, r_!\}_!^{\&}{}_{-\%}, C, d, S\}$$

We evaluate model performance using both the evidence lower bound (ELBO) and the forward simulation accuracy (FSA) (Fig. 3a) described in Nair et al., 2023[91] as well as by calculating the variance explained by the model on data. Briefly, given observed neural activity in the reduced neural state space at time t, we predict the trajectory of population activity over an ensuing small time interval Δt using the fit rSLDS model, then compute the mean squared error (MSE) between that trajectory and the observed data at time t+ Δt. This MSE is computed across all dimensions of the reduced latent space and repeated for all times t across cross validation folds. This error metric is normalized to a 0-1 range in each animal across the whole recording to obtain a bounded measure of model performance. The FSA can intuition of where model performance drops during the recording. In addition to MSE, we also calculate the Pearson's correlation coefficient ($R"$) between the predicted and observed data for each dimension following the forward simulation. By taking the average correlation coefficient across dimensions, we can obtain a quantitative estimate of variance explained by rSLDS on observed data.

The number of states and dimensions used for the model are determined using 5-fold cross validation. Visualization of the dynamical system using principal components analysis is performed as described previously [91].

Code used to fit rSLDS on neural data is available in the SSM package: (https://github.com/lindermanlab/ssm)

Estimation of time constants

We estimated the time constant of each dimension of linear dynamical systems using eigenvalues λ of the dynamics matrix of that system, derived previously[100] as:

$$\tau. = Q^{\dfrac{1}{\log(|\lambda_a|)}}Q$$

Calculation of auto-correlation half-width

We computed autocorrelation halfwidths by calculating the autocorrelation function for each neuron timeseries data (y_t) for a set of lags as described previously[74]. Briefly, for a time series (y_t), the autocorrelation for lag k is:

$$r! = \overline{\dfrac{c!}{c/}}$$

where $c!$ is defined as: 0)!

$$c_l = \frac{1}{T} \sum_{t} W(y_t - \bar{y}Y)(y_{t+1} - \bar{y}Y)$$

and c_l is the sample variance of the data. The half-width is found for each neuron as the point where the autocorrelation function reaches a value of 0.5 (Extended Data Fig.4d-e).

Partial least squares regression to identify integration dynamics

To identify the integration dimension using an independent method, we also used partial least squares regression. Towards this, all traces were concatenated and regressed against a 1 x T vector designed such that the vector shows ramping activity upon entry of the male intruder (see Extended Data Figure 5l, m).

Data availability

The data on which this study is based are available on reasonable request.

Code availability

The custom MATLAB and Python codes used to analyze the data in this study are available on request. Code to rSLDS models is available in the SSM package: https://github.com/lindermanlab/ssm

Acknowledgments: We thank A. Kennedy for critical feedback on the manuscript, Y. Huang for genotyping, G. Mancuso for administrative assistance, C. Chiu for lab management, E. Carcamo for mouse colony management, Caltech OLAR staff for animal care, and members of the Anderson Laboratory for helpful comments on this project. DJA is an investigator of the Howard Hughes Medical Institute. This work was supported by grants from the NIH (RO1MH112593, RO1MH123612 and RO1NS123916). A.N is supported by a National Science Scholarship from the Agency of Science, Technology and Research, Singapore.

Author contributions: Conceptualization: D.J.A., M.L.; Experiments: M.L.; Data analysis: M.L., A.N., S.L.; Supervision: D.J.A.; Writing: D.J.A., M.L., A.N.

Competing interests: Authors declare that they have no competing interests.

Chapter 4

HORMONE DEPENDENT TRANSCRIPTOMIC CHANGES IN FEMALE HYPOTHALAMUS

Summary

To comprehensively compare gene expression patterns in the female hypothalamus at different reproductive states, I conducted sing-cell RNA sequencing (scRNAseq) on the ventral VMH in naturally cycling females during proestrus, diestrus and lactation. The transcriptomic analysis revealed qualitative changes in cell type compositions that showed the absence of one cluster of cells (T-type 3) during diestrus and lactation.

To gain better control over hormones, I performed scRNAseq on the ventral VMH in ovariectomized (OVX) females under hormone-primed and unprimed conditions. The transcriptomic analysis revealed that the cell type composition under OVX unprimed conditions was similar to that observed during naturally cycling diestrus and lactation, with the absence of T-type 3. Interestingly, T-types 1 and 2 were absent under OVX primed conditions.

To investigate the relationship between female mating behaviors and transcriptomic cell types, I conducted activity-dependent scRNAseq on the ventral VMH in OVX primed females after receptive mating and unprimed females after unreceptive mating. I found that the T-type 3 was activated at receptive mating in primed females, while T-type 2 was activated at unreceptive mating in unprimed females.

In summary, these results reveal qualitative transcriptomic changes in the female ventral VMH, dependent on reproductive states. In additional, the state-dependent T-types play a potential role in regulating sexual receptivity in females.

Results

Qualitative changes in transcriptomes of female VMHvl across reproductive states.
To comprehensively compare the gene expression patterns in the female hypothalamus across different reproductive states, I conducted sing-cell RNA sequencing (scRNAseq) on the ventral VMH in naturally cycling virgin females during the proestrus and diestrus states. To enhance control over hormones, I also performed scRNAseq on the ventral VMH in ovariectomized (OVX) females under hormone-primed and unprimed conditions. Subsequently, I integrated this new dataset with a previously collected dataset[6] containing information from data virgin, lactational and post-lactational states (Fig. 1a). The analysis resulted in 27 clusters, consistent with the previous report[6] (Fig. 1a).

Transcriptomic cell type (T-type) analysis across reproductive states revealed significant changes. Comparing naturally cycling virgin females between proestrus and diestrus states revealed the absence of one cluster (T-type 3) during diestrus (Fig. 1b). Comparison among females in lactational, virgin, and post-lactational states revealed the absence of the same cluster (T-type 3) during lactational state. (Fig. 1c).

Comparison in OVX females with or without hormone priming indicated that the cell type composition under OVX unprimed conditions was similar to that in naturally cycling diestrus state, with T-type 3 also absent (Fig. 1d). Interestingly, T-type 1 and 2 were absent in OVX primed conditions (Fig. 1d).

Taken together, these data indicate qualitative changes in female VMHvl transcriptomes across different reproductive states. There is a correlation between the changes in T-types and the state-dependent display of sexual receptivity: with T-type 3 absent during diestrus, lactating and OVX unprimed states, corresponding to periods of an absence of sexual receptivity.

Mating functions of reproductive state-dependent T-types.

To elucidate the functions of VMHvl during receptive and unreceptive mating under varying hormonal states, I conducted a comparative analysis of *c-fos* expression following receptive mating in OVX primed females and unreceptive mating in OVX unprimed females. The results revealed that both receptive and unreceptive mating interactions activated VMHvl, exhibiting similar activity patterns (Fig. 2a).

To further explore the intricate relationship between female mating receptivity and VMHvl transcriptomic cell types, I employed activity-dependent single-cell RNAseq (act-seq) on the ventral VMH in OVX primed females post-receptive mating and OVX unprimed females post-unreceptive mating (Fig. 2b). The analysis demonstrated that a significant activation of T-type 3 following receptive mating in primed females (Fig. 2c), while unreceptive mating in unprimed females significantly activated the T-type 2 (Fig. 2d). Thus, although VMHvl exhibited activation during female mating interactions irrespective of receptivity, distinct Ttypes were activated during receptive and unreceptive mating encounters.

This investigation provides valuable insights into the nuanced functions of reproductive state-dependent T-types within VMHvl, shedding light on the differential neural responses associated with receptive and unreceptive mating interactions.

Differentially expressed genes in reproductive state-dependent T-types.

To discern the distinctions among the identified state dependent T-types, an examination of differentially expressed genes (DEGs) within each T-type in relation to others was conducted. The comparison initially focused on the state-dependent T-types (T-type 3 vs. Ttypes 1&2). Several genes exhibited upregulation in T-type 3, including *Rasl11a* and *Pgr* (Fig. 3a), while others demonstrated downregulation, such as *Cntn5* and *Tac1* (Fig. 3a). Subsequently, a comparison was made between the two unreceptive state T-types exhibiting different activity during mating (T-type 2 vs. T-type 1). DEGs between T-type 1 and 2 indicated potential changes in excitability (Fig. 3b): Mating activated T-type 2 showed a substantial increase in the expression of *Kcnq5*, a member of the KCNQ potassium channel gene family, and *Grik1* (Glutamate Ionotropic Receptor Kainate Type Subunit 1).

Conversely, mating inactivated T-type 1 exhibited notably higher expression of *Gabrg3*, encoding a GABA receptor, and *Kctd8* (Auxiliary subunit of GABA-B receptors).

This comprehensive analysis sheds light on the nuanced molecular profiles associated with distinct reproductive state-dependent T-types, providing valuable insights into the differential regulation of genes involved in excitability and neurotransmission during mating interactions at different hormonal states.

Potential cell type conversion from T-types 1 & 2 to T-type 3

To explore the possibility of cell type conversion among the three reproductive statedependent T-types, a 'Pulse-and-Chase' RNAscope experiment was conducted (Fig. 4a). Given that the reproductive state-dependent T-types 1-3 are α cells labeled by Esr1+, Npy2r, I injected Flpo-on & Cre-off GFP in Esr1-flpo x Npy2r-cre females that were fully OVX and unprimed. Under these conditions, GPF would label T-type 1 and 2 (Fig. 4a, Step 1). The females were then maintained the female in the OVX and unprimed state for 4 weeks until the GFP labeling was fully expressed. Subsequently, the females were hormonally primed, and brain samples were collected immediately upon the entry into the fully primed state, where only T-type 3 was expected (Fig. 4a, Step 2). T-type 3 marker genes were stained in the primed brains, and the co-expression with the labeling GFP was compared (Fig. 4a, Step 3). If T-type 3 cells overlapped with the label GFP+ cells, it suggested a conversion between T-type 3 and 1&2 (Fig. 4a, Result 3).

Rasl11a was chosen as the T-type 3 marker gene, and *Esr1* serving as a control (Fig. 4b). Results indicated selective expression of *Rasl11a* in the primed condition but not in the unprimed condition, while *Esr1* exhibited expression in both conditions (Fig. 4c). Importantly, co-expression of *GFP*, *Rasl11a* and *Esr1* were observed in the primed condition (Fig. 4c). These findings align with the hypothesis that the T-type 1&2 undergo conversion to T-type 3 after hormone priming in OVX females.

Figures

Fig. 1. Qualitative changes in transcriptomes of female VMHvl across reproductive states.

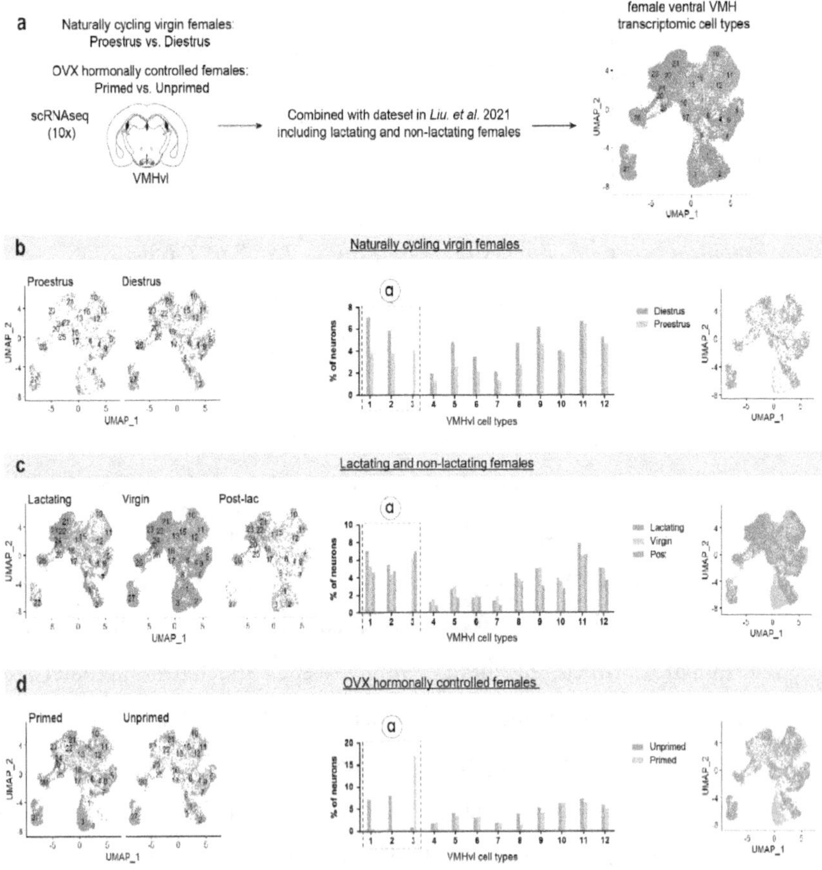

Fig. 1. Qualitative changes in transcriptomes of female VMHvl across reproductive states.

(a) Left, schematic of the scRNA-seq protocol and data integration; Right, UMAP plot colorcoded by clusters identified in tissue dissected from ventral VMH of all females (N=35,656; 27 clusters).

(b-d) UMAP plot and bar plot split by reproductive states identified in tissue dissected from (b) naturally cycling females (N=4,127), (c) lactating and non-lactating females (N=19,356), or (d) OVX hormonally controlled females (N=12,173).

Fig. 2. Mating functions of reproductive state-dependent T-types.

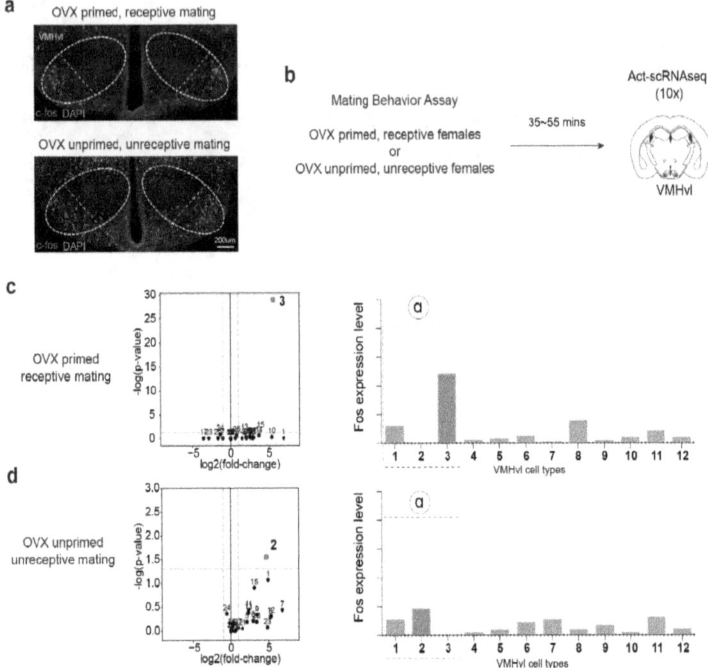

Fig. 2. Mating functions of reproductive state-dependent T-types.

(a) *c-fos* expression pattern in the female VMHvl after receptive mating in OVX primed females, and unreceptive mating in OVX primed females. 'Receptive' is defined by the presence of accepting behaviors, such as lordosis and wiggling during the interaction.

(b) Schematic of the act-seq protocol (N=12,173).

(c-d) Left, "Volcano plots" displaying *Fos* expression levels in 27 VMH cell types from the following animals: (c) OVX primed receptive females, (d) OVX unprimed unreceptive females. Colored dots indicate cell types with *Fos* expression fold change >2 (x axis cut-off) and P <0.05 (y axis cut-off; dashed lines); Right, *Fos* expression levels in 12 VMHvl cell types. Colored bars show T-types with statistically significant increases (fold change >2 & P <0.05) in *Fos* expression relative to no-intruder controls.

Fig. 3. Differentially expressed genes in reproductive state-dependent T-types.

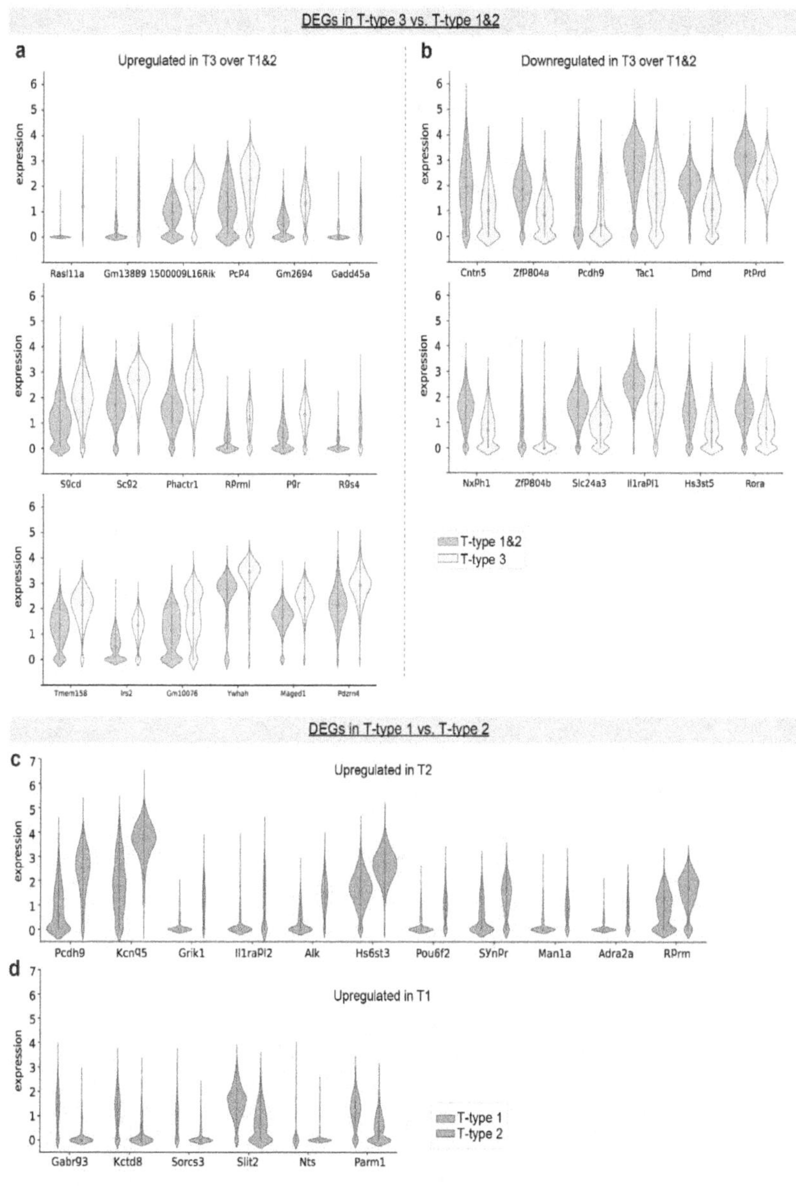

Fig. 3. Differentially expressed genes in reproductive state-dependent T-types. (a-b) Expression levels for genes that are significantly (a) upregulated or (b) downregulated in T-type 3 compared to T-types 1 and 2 (fold change >2 and P <0.05). (c-d) Expression levels for genes that are significantly (a)

upregulated or (b) downregulated in T-type 2 compared to T-type 1 (fold change >2 and P <0.05).

Fig. 4. Potential cell type conversion from T-type 1&2 to 3 via hormone priming.

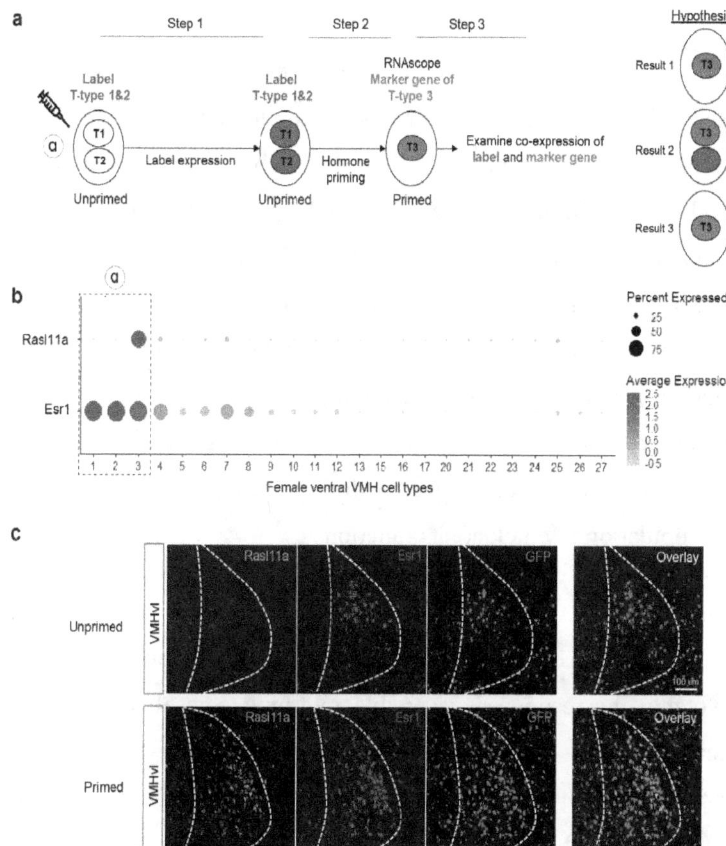

Fig. 4. Potential cell type conversion from T-types 1 & 2 to 3 via hormone priming.

(a) Schematic illustrates the 'pulse-and-chase' experiment.

(b) The expression level of the selected marker gene for T-type 3.

(c) Results of RNAscope staining. Scale bar = 100 um.

FUTURE

Aggression exhibits sexual dimorphism, evident in behaviors, overall circuits, and cell types. Within the VMHvl, a key node in the aggression circuit, one transcriptomic cell type is present and activated by aggression in both males and females. Simultaneously, another Ttype is exclusive to males, activated by male aggression, and absent in females. Unraveling the purpose of this male-specific aggression cell type poses questions: Does it control mating inhibition or contribute to the rewarding component during aggression? Addressing these queries is essential for understanding aggression in both genders. My research, combined with previous studies, has identified genetic markers specific to the male aggression cell type, offering genetic access for imaging and manipulation to elucidate its function.

Female aggression, observed periodically and limited to the lactational state, involves beta cells in VMHvl responding to conspecific cues during lactation. Notably, this response is reversible, returning to baseline after weaning. During pregnancy, the female brain undergoes significant changes with fluctuating hormones such as estrogen, progesterone, and prolactin. Understanding how these hormones modulate circuits, affecting beta cell responses in terms of excitability and connectivity, is crucial for comprehending the underlying processes.

In male aggression, line attractor dynamics are established, but the dynamics of female aggression and how hormones modulate population dynamics remain unclear. Female mating and aggression cells, while distinct, mutually inhibit each other, posing questions about the mechanism of mutual inhibition – potentially involving inhibitory interneurons in the tuberal area or the arcuate nucleus (ARC).

Periodic encoding of female sexual receptivity has been identified, prompting inquiries into how receptivity encoding is modulated within interactions or across the estrus cycle. Neuromodulators' roles and the mechanisms by which they function need exploration. Additionally, the gradual ramping up of female sexual motivation during mating raises questions about its purpose in coordinating with males for a successful and efficient termination of mating. Males display different times for the delay of ejaculation in different strains. This hypothesis can be tested across various strains to examine if the ramping time correlates with the delay of ejaculation in different strains.

Male mating behavior, specifically USV+ mounting, is also observed in females. Activation of MPOA promotes USV+ mounting in both genders, warranting an investigation into its function in females.

I identified the qualitative changes in female VMHvl transcriptomes across distinct reproductive states, revealing a correlation between T-type alterations, hormonal states, and behavioral receptivity. Specifically, T-type 3 is conspicuously absent during diestrus, lactational and OVX unprimed states, coinciding with the observed absence of sexual receptivity during these periods.

Building on our previous understanding that VMHvl α cells causally control female receptivity, and they formed line-attractor dynamics during mating, occurring in a reproductive-state dependent manner, the identification of DEGs in these cell types adds a layer of complexity to our understanding. Considering the potential links between changes in gene expression patterns and neural dynamics, our findings pave the way for future investigations. For example, does the emergence of T-type 3 contribute to the line attractor dynamics in the receptive state? Alternatively, do the genes upregulated in T-type 3 contribute to the persistent features? These results are poised to contribute significantly to unraveling the cellular and molecular mechanisms that underlie hormonal state-dependent regulation of population dynamics in female VMHvl, and ultimately shedding light on their impacts on mating behaviors.

In summary, this study lays the foundation for a more comprehensive understanding of the intricate interplay between reproductive states, gene expression, and neural dynamics in the female social-sexual circuits.